# From Language to Creative Writing: An Introduction

Philip Seargeant and
Bill Greenwell

BLOOMSBURY ACADEMIC

First published in 2013 by

Bloomsbury Publishing Plc
50 Bedford Square
London WC1B 3DP
www.bloomsbury.com

in association with

The Open University
Walton Hall, Milton Keynes
MK7 6AA
United Kingdom

ISBN 978 1 408 17521 7

A CIP catalogue record for this book is available from the British Library

Available in the USA from Bloomsbury Academic & Professional,
175 Fifth Avenue/3rd Floor, New York, NY 10010.

Typeset by Margaret Brain

This publication is based on the book *Identity and Expression*, which forms part of the Open University module A150 *Voices and Texts*. Details of this and other Open University modules can be obtained from the Student Registration and Enquiry Service, The Open University, PO Box 197, Milton Keynes MK7 6BJ, United Kingdom (+44 (0)845 300 60 90, email general-enquiries@open.ac.uk, www.open.ac.uk).

This book is produced using paper that is made from wood grown in managed, sustainable forests. It is natural, renewable and recyclable. The logging and manufacturing processes conform to the environmental regulations of the country of origin.

# Contents

# List of tables and figures

# Acknowledgements

Every effort has been made to trace copyright holders and we apologise in advance for any unintentional omission. We would be pleased to insert the appropriate acknowledgement in any subsequent edition.

Grateful acknowledgments are due as follows:

Extract from 'Mother Tongue'. Copyright © 1990 by Amy Tan. First appeared in *The Threepenny Review*. Reprinted by permission of the author and the Sandra Dijkstra Literary Agency. Permission to reprint also granted by the Abner Stein agency.

Extract from *English with an Accent* by Rosina Lippi-Green © 1997 Routledge. Reproduced by permission of Taylor & Francis Books UK.

Extract from *The Stories of English* by David Crystal (Allen Lane, 2004) Copyright © David Crystal, 2004. Reproduced by permission of Penguin Books Ltd.

Extract from *Genre Analysis, English in Academic and Research Settings* by John Swales (1990). Copyright © Cambridge University Press 1990, reproduced with permission.

Extract from *Speech Genres and Other Late Essays* by M. M. Bakhtin, translated by Vern W. McGee, edited by Caryl Emerson and Michael Holquist, Copyright © 1986. Courtesy of the University of Texas Press.

Extract from 'Institutional Discourse' by Celia Roberts, from: *Routledge Companion to English Language Studies*, edited by J. Maybin, copyright © 2010 Routledge. Reproduced by permission of Taylor & Francis Books UK.

Extract from the script of *The Smoking Room* by Brian Dooley (2004) reproduced by kind permission of the author.

Extract from 'Language, reality and power' by Norman Fairclough, in Culpeper, J., Katamba, F., Kerswill, P., Wodak, R. and McEnery, T. (eds) *English Language: Description, Variation and Context* (2009, Palgrave Macmillan), reproduced with permission of Palgrave Macmillan.

Extract from Caryl Churchill's *Three More Sleepless Nights* in *Shorts* (Nick Hern Books, 1990). *Churchill Shorts* © 1990 by Caryl Churchill. www.nickhernbooks.co.uk. Reproduced with permission from Nick Hern Books.

# Introduction: from language to creative writing

## From communication to expression

At one point in Jonathan Swift's novel *Gulliver's Travels* the hero finds himself in a city called Lagado, where he is given a tour of a scientific academy. There he is shown a number of innovative projects for the betterment of mankind. These include such bizarre things as a device for extracting sunbeams from cucumbers, and a radical new method of architecture intended to revolutionise the building of houses 'by beginning at the Roof and working downwards to the Foundation' (2003 [1726], p. 168). At the academy's School of Language, he is introduced to a scheme for 'entirely abolishing Words altogether' (p. 172). Instead of speaking, people will simply carry around all the objects they are likely to want to refer to, and then produce them one by one when they wish to 'say' anything. The only apparent drawback is that if one wants to have an extended conversation, the collection of objects one needs to carry around becomes very cumbersome. As Gulliver comments:

> I have often beheld two of those Sages almost sinking under the Weight of their Packs, like Peddlers amongst us; who when they met in the Streets would lay down their Loads, open their Sacks and hold Conversation for an Hour together; then put up their Implements, help each other to resume their Burthens, and take their Leave.
>
> (Swift, 2003 [1726], pp. 172–4)

The underlying principle of this scheme is that 'Words are only Names for *Things*' (p. 172). Swift's novel is a satire, and in this episode he is parodying the world of science and academia. But although he is obviously mocking this as a workable system of communication, the core conception of language that underpins this idea – the notion that 'words are names for things' – is actually a very popular and widespread one. The idea that languages consist of vast hoards of words, all of which stand for something out there in the world, and that their main purpose is to relay factual information, is not at all uncommon.

Human language is far more multi-faceted than this, however. The eighteenth-century German thinker Wilhelm von Humboldt wrote that human language is a system which 'makes infinite use of finite means' (quoted in Chomsky, 1965, p. v). That is, from a palette of basic sounds (vowels and consonants), or from the relatively small group of letters which make up the alphabet, we are able to put together complex sentences which can articulate an infinite number of things. Furthermore, language does not *only* represent objects out there in the world. It expresses feelings, ideas, emotions and aspects of identity, and is also used as a form of action which helps us get things done. How from a bundle of objects carried around on one's back would one be able to say 'I'm sorry about that', or 'Would you mind if we take a rain check and reschedule for next Thursday', let alone express the range of feelings that can be achieved in a sonnet or a song?

The subject of this book is the ways in which language works to express this variety of feelings, ideas and emotions, and how we can draw on its resources for creative writing. The book has two central topics: the nature of language and the practice of writing. Language is the raw material from which all texts are constructed. Writing is the process by which this raw material is converted into coherent works of cultural expression. It is the imaginative act which turns words and ideas into works of linguistic creativity. The book therefore looks at how language is used, both in everyday life and in literature, and at the range of skills and strategies we can use to manipulate it in the process of creative writing.

## From observation to invention

With its focus on the two fundamental elements involved in the creation of written texts, the book brings together what are usually treated as two different subjects: Language Studies and Creative Writing.

Language Studies – or, as the discipline is often more formally known, Linguistics – has as its main focus the theoretical analysis of human language and language use. In other words, it looks at how languages are structured, what they are used for, and how they have evolved. For many people, language is considered an essential element of what it means to be human. For example, the Renaissance dramatist Ben Jonson wrote that language is 'the only benefit man hath to expresse his excellencie of mind above other creatures' (1947 [1641], pp. 620–1). Given the important and complex role that language plays in the human experience, the discipline of Linguistics is naturally a very broad one. For our purposes, we will concentrate primarily on the ways in which language functions as a fundamental resource by means of which people express their ideas and identities, and through which they interact with the social world around them. In the chapters which focus primarily on Language Studies (see the explanation of the structure of the book below), we will look at the use of language – and specifically the English language – in the creation of texts and communicative acts in a variety of different contexts. And we will consider the range of ways that language gives us for expressing our experience of the world. In doing this we will examine examples from everyday language use, as well as from the media and literature.

The second discipline the book draws on is Creative Writing. In formal educational settings, such as university, this is a relatively new academic subject. That is to say, although people have engaged in acts of creative writing since the beginning of human civilisation, it is only in the last thirty years or so that it has been regularly taught as a distinct university subject. As an activity, however, writing is absolutely central to our social existence. So many aspects of our everyday life involve some sort of writing, be it scribbling out a shopping list, sending emails, or preparing documents for work. In this respect we are all already 'writers'.

'Creative' writing is, of course, a slightly different type of activity to most of the writing we engage in on a daily basis. It is one which draws on the imagination of the writer, and which uses structures and strategies to engage the imagination of a reader. In the Creative Writing chapters of the book you will have the opportunity to explore and experiment with a number of writing strategies, and to engage in the crafting of language to create short pieces of both prose and poetry.

We noted at the beginning of this section that the two subjects are usually studied separately, and are seen as having different methods and different goals. But although Language Studies conventionally tends to analyse other people's language use while Creative Writing tends to play with one's own use of language, they should not be seen as mutually exclusive. And while Language Studies is often viewed as an 'empirical social science', i.e. something which relies on objective observation and analysis of real-life phenomena, and Creative Writing is seen as a 'practice-based art', as the linguist Rob Pope observes, 'ultimately – for all their differences of object, aim and methodology – both deal with language experientially as well as experimentally, and both engage in kinds of discovery and intervention' (Pope, 2010, p. 132). In other words, both Language Studies and Creative Writing draw on our experience of language use and our desire to investigate its workings and potential.

This book purposely approaches the two disciplines as complementary, and is based on the principle that the study of language can help inform the practice of creative writing. But we are also suggesting that the experience and practice of creative writing can inform an understanding of language and the way that it works. Looking at the processes involved in writing gives an insightful perspective into the nature of other people's texts, and allows us to consider them not solely from the point of view of the reader or audience, but from that of the writer as well.

## The structure of the book

The book is structured around two interwoven strands. Chapter 1 outlines the nature of the two disciplines in more detail, and explains the principles behind their use in the book. Thereafter, the chapters alternate between those focusing on Language Studies and those on Creative Writing. They are grouped in such a way that the issues introduced in one chapter complement those in the next. Throughout the book therefore we will be making links between the two disciplines, and aiming to explore how approaching a text from both an analytic and creative perspective can help us appreciate the way that we actively engage with words whenever we use language.

The chapters also include readings by other writers which discuss the concepts or issues we are examining, or provide illustrations of the types of writing we are looking at. In addition, there are activities interwoven throughout the book which give you the opportunity to reflect upon and engage with the topics being introduced. Finally, there is a glossary at the end which gives definitions of all the technical terms used in the book.

# 1 The study of language and the practice of creative writing

In this chapter we look in more depth at what the disciplines of Language Studies and Creative Writing involve: what it is they study and how they go about studying it.

## The study of language in use

In the Language Studies chapters we will be looking at ways in which we can analyse language – and specifically the English language – and how people use English as part of everyday life. As noted in the Introduction, language is an intrinsic part of human experience, and because of this, it can be studied from a number of different perspectives. The study of language includes such diverse issues as:

1. the structure of languages – that is, the specific grammatical rules that govern the composition of sentences in different languages

2. how the brain processes language – in other words, what goes on inside your brain when you use language

3. how people acquire languages – either learning them from infancy, or studying them later in life

4. how language is used for creative or persuasive purposes, as, for example, in the composition of poetry or public speeches.

Each of these perspectives is a branch of the general discipline of **Linguistics**. In the book, however, we will be looking predominantly at the way people *use* language, and at how that usage is influenced by the society they live in and the social interactions they take part in. This approach is known broadly as **sociolinguistics**. The focus here is on the relationship between language use and social structures. It is an approach that examines the ways in which people use language, what they use it for, and how this use is influenced by their social circumstances and environment. If this all sounds rather abstract and theoretical at the moment, don't worry because throughout the book we will be looking at several examples of actual language use and discussing exactly what the relationship is between language and society.

Let's begin by making a simple but fundamental point. When we speak we communicate both by what we say (the content of our **utterances**) and by how we say it (the form those utterances take). As soon as someone speaks even a couple of words to us, we begin to make judgements about their identity – where they're from, what sort of education they have had, what their social background is, and so on. Chapters 2 and 4 will examine what it is about the way we speak that allows people to infer all this information. We will be looking at how our use of language is influenced by the environment from which we come or in which we live (that is, our social surroundings), and how important this context is for the way that we communicate with each other.

---

## A note on terminology

The word 'utterance' as used in the paragraph above simply means a complete unit of speech that someone uses when speaking. Such a unit of speech will often be preceded and followed by a space of silence, or by a change of speaker. It could be a whole sentence, a string of sentences, or just a single word ('Help' or 'no'), or possibly even a half-spoken word or meaningful sound ('Erm …'). As you can see, this meaning is slightly different from the colloquial use of the word.

As with most disciplines, Linguistics uses several technical terms, and this is one of them. These technical terms help to describe in a detailed and exact way the phenomena that Linguistics studies. The glossary at the end of the book has a list of definitions of all the words that are highlighted in bold.

---

Throughout the Language Studies chapters we will be looking both at spoken and written language, though with a rough division between the earlier and later chapters: Chapters 3 and 5 look predominantly at examples from spoken **discourse**, while Chapters 7 and 9 look more at the written use of language. (The word 'discourse' here simply means a sequence of connected speech or writing.) Dividing the book in this way allows us to look at the two fundamental forms language takes (speech and writing); but it also raises something of a paradox. This is that, despite the fact I've just stated that the earlier chapters will be focusing predominantly on spoken language, what you have in front of you is a book consisting entirely of writing (plus the occasional image). So, even before we start, we are confronted with the paradox that the examples about the spoken form of the language will be represented in the book by means of the written language.

What does it mean, then, to say that something that is very obviously a line of squiggles printed on a piece of paper (i.e. is very clearly 'writing') is an example of 'spoken' language? The answer concerns the fact that the way people *structure* what they write or say is an integral part of the communicative message they convey. Spoken language often has a distinctively different structure from written language. And differences in structure are not just to be found in the distinction between spoken and written discourse. A dialect that is spoken in one part of the UK will have a different internal structure to that spoken in another part. How people structure language in different ways is a complex and multifaceted process, yet it is something that happens automatically (and often unconsciously) in any instance of communication, and that is picked up on instantly by recipients of the message. The Language Studies chapters will introduce you to this complexity, and to the crucial roles that language plays in our everyday lives as social beings.

## Creative writing: purpose and process

While Language Studies is a discipline about observation and analysis, Creative Writing is more about process: you cannot study it unless you try it, not least because the aim is to reflect on your writing at the planning stage, during composition and when you have finished.

As with its near-neighbour Literary Studies, Creative Writing includes looking at existing texts. To a certain extent, it also analyses them. But the purpose of the analysis is quite different: it is to give you ideas of how you might write your own material; to give you a sense of what might or might not work for you as a writer; to understand the dynamic of writing in action. On a Creative Writing course you read a wide range of texts in order to think about strategies and tactics, rather than to analyse content and intention. In other words, it is about reading so that you can find and hone your own style, and about finding and honing the voices of the characters and speakers you create. The examples of other people's writing will also give you reference points by which to analyse your own work.

As a discipline, Creative Writing asks you to create stories or sequences of images, and to work through the best ways of engaging a reader or **audience**. It asks you to look at generating ideas, and teaches you ways of refining language and structure so that these narratives or sequences have a maximum impact. One of the most important processes consists of **drafting** and editing what you have written, considering alternative ways of phrasing, and making decisions about such questions as what you need to leave in or leave out, and how best to sharpen the focus of what you write.

A good illustration of how editing can be used to sharpen the focus of a narrative is the experience of making a film. Whether for reasons of economy or for dramatic effect, film-makers rapidly learn how much they can leave out. If a film-maker wants us to know that a character is going from one place to another, for example, it may be tempting to give us the whole of the journey. However, if we see a character going in through the front door of an apartment block, say, on the way to an upstairs apartment, we do not need to see the character travelling up the stairs. In fact, we might not need to see the character going through the apartment door. Instead, a film-maker might simply take us directly from outside the front door to inside the apartment. The person inside might hear a rap on the door. Opening the door would reveal the character at the head of a stairwell. That would be enough to tell us that the character had made the journey. This kind of 'cut' is increasingly common in stories – and prose fiction has itself been much influenced by film.

Given that Creative Writing is about putting these ideas into practice rather than simply reading about them, let's conclude this introduction to the discipline with an activity. To get you used to the process of editing, the activity below asks you to edit a short and uninspiring piece of writing so that it is economical.

---

## ACTIVITY

Read the following passage, which I have invented, and which I have deliberately over-written. See how far you can edit it so that what happens is clear without having to be spelled out – that is, so that the content **shows** what is happening, rather than **tells**. You should aim to reduce it by 80 to 90 words, and, above all, make it more interesting. You may change or reorder any of the words, but keep the gist of the passage intact:

> Molly spread two slices of toast with raspberry jam, went over to the breakfast table, sat down in a chair, and ate them. She looked through the window: it was a sunny morning, and it looked as if it would be a sweltering day, just as the weather forecast had predicted. Her husband, who was a gruff and surly type, sat opposite her, sucking his teeth in annoyance at some item he was reading in the daily newspaper, which they had delivered from the local shop. He read out some extracts. He was an arrogant man, the complete opposite of Molly, who was sensitive and lively, and who would have preferred a brighter conversation.
>
> The phone rang in the next room, and Molly got up, went over to the door, opened it, and answered it. It was her daughter, Shelagh, who had important and

very shocking news to tell. Her house had been burgled the previous night, and some valuable jewellery had been stolen by the thief or thieves, including a locket which contained a picture of Molly's mother. Molly's mother had passed away twenty years earlier, but her memory seemed very fresh in Molly's mind. She was instantly upset, but let her garrulous daughter explain all the details of the break-in, which had happened, so her daughter said, when she had been asleep. Molly asked her, when she could get a word in, whether the police had been called.

## DISCUSSION

There are many examples in this piece of what could be termed poor or clumsy writing, although the most glaring problem, I think, is the absence of **dialogue**. The passage is uninhabited by the voices of characters, even if the husband is 'a gruff and surly type' – something we would have realised if we had heard him speak. We are also told that he is 'arrogant', something it would have been more interesting to find out for ourselves. Equally, we did not have to be told either that Molly is 'sensitive and lively' and later that she is 'upset', or that the daughter is 'garrulous'. We could have gleaned that from an excerpt of conversation or a description of behaviour. We are told about the weather, when we could have had it suggested; we are told pointless details, such as the process of sitting down, the method of the newspaper delivery, the process of going to the next room, and even that the news is 'shocking', which paradoxically robs the news of any shock. We are also told what happens in a relentlessly chronological order, and given an indigestible chunk of **back-story** (about Molly's mother). There is also some confusion about to whom the personal pronoun 'she' refers (there are three women mentioned), and there is an unfortunate sequence of phrasing in the very first sentence, which makes it seem as if the chair and table are being eaten.

There are plenty of solutions, and one of the pleasures of writing is that there is no perfectly right answer. Perhaps the best thing to do would be to cut straight to the conversation between mother and daughter. The opening line might be Molly saying 'What did they take?' That would at least force us to read on. Bringing a voice into a creative text is a good way of enlivening it – and it is this notion of 'voice' which we will explore in Chapter 3.

---

Having outlined what it is the two disciplines focus on and – equally importantly – how it is they go about investigating and engaging with their objects of study, let's now move to these objects of study themselves. We will begin, in the next chapter, by looking at how language use is related to identity.

# 2 Speech and dialect

## Diversity and identity

Central to the study of the relationship between language and society is what is known as **language variation**. This is the principle that the language people speak is variable – that the way it sounds and the way it is structured will vary depending on the person using it and the circumstances in which it is used. And this variation is a key factor in the way that language acts as a marker of identity. We can illustrate this with a simple exercise.

---

### ACTIVITY

Look at the three short utterances below. Each is a different way of saying 'Thank you'. Based solely on these simple phrases, what assumptions can you make about the type of people who might use them? What age, or social or geographical background, do you think people using these different phrases might have?

> Example 1: 'Thanks awfully'
>
> Example 2: 'Cheers mate'
>
> Example 3: 'Ta love'.

### DISCUSSION

This is, of course, a rather speculative exercise. But to me, Example 1 sounds like the sort of thing that is likely to be used by someone from an upper-middle-class background, and probably from an older generation. Example 2 has a younger feel to it. I wouldn't associate it with any particular class, but it sounds colloquial, and possibly suggests a male rather than female speaker. Example 3 has associations with the north of England for me. Again, there is a colloquial feel to it, and if I had to guess, I'd say this person was probably from a lower-middle or working-class background. All three have quite a British ring to them, though Example 2 could possibly also be used by someone from Australia or New Zealand.

As I say, this is hardly a scientific exercise. But the point to note is that even from simple two-word utterances like these we can make basic assumptions about the type of people who might use them. Each of these phrases has the same function – they are all expressions of gratitude – and yet they each consist of a different combination of words. And it is because of this combination of words that we are able to infer a meaning both about what the speaker was trying to express (a sense of gratitude), and about their identity.

---

As you can see from the activity then, it is possible to make some rough inferences about a person's identity from even the most basic evidence of their linguistic habits. The reason we are able to do this is because people don't all use language the same way. We often talk of 'English' as a single entity. In sentences such as 'English is my native language', or '*Great Expectations* is a novel written in English' or 'She's been learning English for five years now', we refer simply to a general concept called 'English'. But when we start to look at the language closely, and to examine in detail how people use it, we begin to see that there is a great deal of diversity on display. Far from being one unchanging system which everyone who speaks the language has knowledge of and access to in equal measure, English as it is actually used represents a bewilderingly wide range of different forms and incarnations. For instance, the 'English' that I speak is different from the English in a Charles Dickens novel, or from that spoken by a university student studying the language in Beijing. Examples from all three would still be very recognisably 'English'; but at the same time, they would be distinct enough for us to start noticing patterns in their usage which could be used to differentiate between them.

This diversity in the language occurs on a number of different levels. Part of it happens on an entirely individual basis. When we speak or write we make sounds in the airwaves or marks on a piece of paper that are unique to us. For this reason, it is possible to recognise someone whom you know well simply from the sound of their voice or the shape of their handwriting. In this respect, the sound of their voice is as unique to them as their facial features, and their handwriting is as much a part of them as their mannerisms or posture. But this individuality in language use is not restricted to the physical means used to produce speech or writing. It is also possible to recognise someone you know well from their turn of phrase or from particular expressions they favour. In other words, the way an individual organises the words and phrases he or she uses is also distinct, and everyone does it slightly differently.

Just as we can recognise individuals from the distinctive way they use language, it is also possible to identify their relationship to wider groups within society by their use of language. This is because we often use language in a similar way to the people around us, and because different groups develop different patterns of usage. At the most noticeable level this happens in the way different *national* groups use different languages. For example, the French as a group use a different language from Italians. Several centuries ago, their ancestors spoke varieties of the same language (Latin), but as their group identities evolved – and as the politics of that region of Europe gradually changed – the single language slowly altered into separate languages, which now have different names and resemble each other only very slightly. And this same phenomenon happens on far smaller scales as well, and occurs within communities whose members nominally speak the same language. As a general principle, language variation occurs according to the different ways people are grouped in society. This may be according to their geographical location, their social class, or other factors such as gender. In each case, the associations we have with the people around us are reflected in the way we use language, and this in turn becomes an aspect of our identity as part of that group.

## Dialect and accent

Let's now look in more detail at two particular ways in which speech differs from group to group. The first of these is **accent**, which refers to the ways in which people pronounce the words they speak.

---

### ACTIVITY

Look at the five couplets below. They are all from poems written in English. Most are by well-known writers, while one is a traditional folk-rhyme. Take a moment to read them aloud and then jot down which of the lines rhyme when you speak them. If you have a chance to ask someone who has a different geographical background to you, get them to try the activity as well, and then compare your results.

1. Put this hat on your head, it will keep your head warm;
   Take a sweet kiss, it will do you no harm.

2. The jay makes answer as the magpie chatters;
   And all the air is filled with pleasant noise of waters.

3. If they call you 'pretty maid', and chuck you 'neath the chin,
   Don't you tell where no one is, nor yet where no one's been!

4. He glows with all the spirit of the Bard,
   Fame, honest fame, his great, his dear reward.

5. My mother groaned, my father wept,
   Into the dangerous world I leapt.

## DISCUSSION

Depending on where you're from, you may have thought that one or maybe two of these rhyme but the others don't. For me, brought up in London and speaking with a standard south-east-England accent, the only one which actually rhymes is Couplet 5. In all the others, the vowel sounds of the words at the end of each line are different. For example, although the words 'Bard' and 'reward' in Couplet 4 both end in '-ard', when I pronounce them the first is more of an 'ahh' sound, and the second more of an 'or' sound. This particular couplet is from a poem by Robert Burns called 'The Brigs of Ayr', which is written in Scots, the language variety traditionally spoken in Lowland Scotland (Smith, 1996). Couplet 1 is from 'The Juniper Tree', a traditional children's folk-rhyme from the American Midwest – Eastern Illinois, to be precise (Van Doren, 1919). Couplet 2 is from a poem by William Wordsworth called 'Resolution and Independence'. This is in a Cumbrian accent, reflecting the speech of the part of the country where Wordsworth was born and lived for much of his life. Couplet 3 is from a poem by Rudyard Kipling called 'A Smuggler's Song'; it's written in a Sussex dialect and is an imitation of the speech of the community along the south coast of England where smugglers operated. And finally, Couplet 5 is from 'Infant Sorrow' by William Blake. Blake was born and lived his early life in London. This couplet rhymes in a standard British English accent.

---

Many people think that accents are what *other* people have. They believe that they speak their native language without any accent, and that theirs is the neutral, natural way to pronounce the language. But as the linguist John Esling writes:

> The fact is that everyone has an accent. It tells other people who we are because it reflects the places we have been and the things we have done. But the construct of accent, like so many other things, is relative. We may only realise that others think we have an accent when we leave the place we came from and find ourselves among people who share a different background from our own, or when a newcomer to our local area stands out as having a distinctly different pronunciation from most of those in our group – that is, relative to us.
>
> (Esling, 1998, p. 169)

As the activity above shows, though, when different accents are placed side by side, it is quite clear that our own way of pronouncing words is only one of many alternatives. What the sociolinguistic study of language does is survey and describe different pronunciations by looking at the **phonology** of the language – that is, the way its system of sounds is organised (see text box below). Sociolinguists also observe how these differences form patterns in the way that particular groups speak, and they relate these patterns to a number of different social categories. The sociolinguist Peter Stockwell contends that 'Accent can often tell us where someone comes from, their age, gender, level of education, social class, wealth, how well-travelled they are, and whether they are emotionally attached to their home-town, job or political party' (2002, p. 7).

---

## Phonology

Phonology is the term used for the study of the sound system of a language. As is often remarked upon, the relationship between the way that English is written and the way it's pronounced is not always straightforward. English spelling does not systematically represent the sound of words; a fact that can cause a fair amount of difficulty for anyone trying to learn English as a foreign language. In many instances, the same sound can be represented by different combinations of letters (e.g. practi**c**e and practi**s**e), while conversely, the same letter or letters can be pronounced in a number of different ways (e.g. **ch**ord and **ch**ortle). And, as we have seen above, the same word can be pronounced in different ways in different accents.

Because of this, sociolinguists who wish to accurately represent spoken language use a specialised form of notation called the **International Phonetic Alphabet (IPA)**. The IPA uses symbols which each represent one fixed sound, so they can be used to accurately transcribe the way that any utterance actually sounds. We won't be using the IPA in this book because it provides a level of detail that is unnecessary for our present purposes. But it is worth remembering that the relationship between the conventional alphabet and the speech sounds of English is not one of exact and stable representation. We'll revisit this issue in the last chapter of the book when we look at how the sounds of a language can be manipulated for poetic purposes.

---

An important related issue to the different accents that people speak with is how those accents are evaluated by other people. We'll return to look at this later in the chapter. Before doing so, let's look at the other major way in which language variation manifests itself: **dialect**.

Whereas 'accent' refers specifically to the way people pronounce the language, 'dialect' refers to the patterns of variation in vocabulary and **grammar**. There are two broad types of dialect: regional and social. A regional dialect is the distinctive pattern of usage that occurs in a community located in a particular geographical location. A social dialect is a variety shared by people of the same class, social status or educational background. Often the two are combined. For example, a person can speak a working-class Cockney dialect – that is, speak in a way that is distinctive of working-class communities living in the London area.

In popular usage the word 'dialect' is often used to mean 'regional' or 'non-standard' dialect, and as such it can have pejorative connotations. A common assumption is that the **standard language** (i.e. the one most often used in the media, in education, and in most official contexts) is the *correct* version, and that other varieties are imperfect renditions of this. But in sociolinguistics, *any* variety of language is a dialect. In other words, just as we all have an accent, so we also all speak in a particular dialect. From a purely linguistic point of view, all dialects are equal. There is nothing in the way they are individually structured that makes one better or worse than another. They are simply different. From a *social* point of view, however, dialects are not all equal, and we'll look at why this is the case in Chapter 4. First, though, let's look at some examples of dialect features from around the English-speaking world.

Dialectal difference can be found in almost all aspects of the grammar and vocabulary of a language, including things such as word order, the way different tenses are formed in verbs, and the choice of vocabulary. We'll concentrate here on two particular areas: the use of pronouns, and different vocabularies.

In modern standard English, the personal pronoun 'you' is used to refer to both single and plural subjects. If I say something like, 'Could you please come over here?' it's not possible to tell from the grammar of the sentence alone whether I'm addressing one person or several. This was not always the case though. As is still the case in many European languages, English used to make a distinction here, with the word 'thou' used for the singular and 'you' for the plural. Over the centuries, however, this distinction slowly disappeared from standard English. 'You' began to be used both for the plural and as a polite term for referring to individual people – in the same way that 'vous' is in French – and gradually the polite form entirely replaced the basic singular 'thou' (Trudgill, 1999, p. 85).

In many regional English dialects a distinction between the singular and plural is still made. In dialects around Liverpool and certain parts of the north-east of England, for example, the pronoun 'youse' (pronounced so as to rhyme with the verb 'use') will be used when referring to more than one person (see Table 1). In the southern states of the USA, the pronoun 'yall' is common, while in the Pittsburgh area of Philadelphia people use the pronoun 'yinz'. As the sociolinguist Kevin Watson notes, while some people may consider these pronouns to be misuses of proper English and thus in some way inferior, 'the non-standard dialects are actually doing a "better job" here than the standard variety because they make a contrast, like many other European languages, which standard English cannot without adding a phrase like *you guys*' (2009, p. 347).

**Table 1**   Plural second-person pronouns in English

|  | Standard English | Liverpool and the north-east of England | Southern US English | Pittsburgh |
|---|---|---|---|---|
| 2nd person singular | Are you coming? | Are you coming? | Are you coming? | Are you coming? |
| 2nd person plural | Are you coming? | Are youse coming? | Are yall coming? | Are yinz coming? |

Source: Watson (2009, p. 347)

Another key area in which dialects differ is in terms of vocabulary. The dialect specialist Peter Trudgill gives the example of different words used across the UK for 'very' (1990, p. 104). So the phrase 'It's very tasty' could be spoken in the following different ways in different parts of the country:

It's *right* tasty (Central North)

It's *well* tasty (Home Counties)

It's *gey* tasty (Northumberland)

It's *gradely* tasty (Lancashire)

That's *wholly* tasty (Eastern Counties)

It be *main* tasty (Wiltshire and Hampshire)

## ACTIVITY

Read the following extracts from well-known works of literature, all of which use a specific dialect of English as a way of indicating something about the geographical or social milieu in which the characters live. As you read each extract, think about the following questions:

1. What particular aspects of the language appear to be non-standard dialect features?

2. Do any of these authors represent accent as well as dialect, and if so, how?

3. Do you have any idea of where these dialects are from?

### Extract 1

I was powerful lazy and comfortable – didn't want to get up and cook breakfast. Well, I was dozing off again, when I thinks I hears a sounds of 'boom!' away up the river. I rouses up and rests on my elbow and listens; pretty soon I hears it again. I hopped up and went and looked out at a hole in the leaves, and I see a bunch of smoke laying on the water a long ways up – about abreast the ferry. And there was the ferry-boat full of people, floating along down. I knowed what was the matter, now. 'Boom!' I see the white smoke squirt out of the ferry-boat's side. You see, they was firing cannon over the water, trying to make my carcass come to the top.

### Extract 2

*(Village roadside. Martin is sitting near the forge, cutting sticks.)*

TIMMY:     Let you make haste out there. I'll be putting up new fires at the turn of day, and you haven't the half of them cut yet.

MARTIN:    It's destroyed I'll be whacking your old thorns till the turn of day, and I with no food in my stomach would keep the life of a pig. Let you come out here and cut them yourself if you want them cut, for there's an hour every day when a man has a right to his rest.

TIMMY:     Do you want me to be driving you off again to be walking the roads? There you are now, and I giving you your food, and a corner to sleep, and money with it; and, to hear the talk of you, you'd think I was after beating you, or stealing your gold.

### Extract 3

THE MAN:   I'll tell you why. Fust: I'm intelligent – ff ff f! it's rotten cold here – yes: intelligent beyond the station o life into which it has pleased the capitalist to call me; and they dont like a man that sees through em. Second, an intelligent bein needs a doo share of appiness; so I drink something cruel when I get the chawnce. Third, I stand by my class and do as little as I can so's to leave arf the job for me fellow workers. Fourth, I'm fly enough to know wots inside the law and wots outside it; and inside it I do as the capitalists do: pinch what I can lay me hands on. In a proper state of society I am sober, industrious and honest: in

> Rome, so to speak, I do as the Romans do. Wots the consequence? When trade is bad – and it's rotten bad just now – and the employers az to sack arf their men, they generally start on me.

## DISCUSSION

Extract 1 is a passage from Mark Twain's *Huckleberry Finn* (1999 [1884], p. 35). In the preface to the novel, Twain writes that:

> In this book a number of dialects are used, to wit: the Missouri Negro dialect; the extremest form of the backwoods South-Western dialect; the ordinary 'Pike-County' dialect; and four modified variations of this last. The shadings have not been done in a haphazard fashion, or by guess-work; but painstakingly, and with the trustworthy guidance and support of personal familiarity with these several forms of speech.
>
> (Twain, 1999 [1884], p. 2)

In other words, although this is an artistic representation of dialect rather than a naturally occurring piece of discourse, Twain has attempted to accurately replicate features of the speech of the communities in which the novel is set. And he has done this both in terms of vocabulary choice and grammatical structure. A couple of features that you might have noticed in this passage are the use of the intensifier 'powerful' rather than 'very' in the phrase 'I was *powerful* lazy'; and the use of the non-standard verb form 'knowed' instead of 'knew' for the simple past tense in the phrase 'I *knowed* what was the matter'. Features such as these are part of the distinctive voice that the author creates for the narrator here. (We will be discussing the creation of different 'voices' in more detail in the next chapter.)

Extract 2 is from a play called *The Well of the Saints* by the Irish dramatist J.M. Synge (1981 [1905], p. 147). The action of the play is set in rural County Wicklow in the east of Ireland, and there are a number of features of 'Irish English' in the characters' speech. One notable example here is the use of what is known as 'it-clefting'. This is a syntactic structure in which a single verb phrase is broken into two phrases by the addition of the word 'it' (Harris, 1993). In standard English, for example, we might say 'I'll be destroyed', but in this extract Martin says 'It's destroyed I'll be'. Another common feature in Irish English is the use of 'after' plus the '-ing' form of a verb as a way of indicating the immediate past (Hickey, 2007). This is used in the extract when Timmy says 'you'd think I was after beating you'. Again, features such as these contribute to the way that the characters' identities are represented.

Finally, Extract 3 is from George Bernard Shaw's play *Major Barbara* (1960 [1907]). The action in this scene is set in West Ham, in the East End of London. In this extract, Shaw is representing both a working-class East End dialect and an accent. He represents the accent by using non-standard spelling for many of the words the characters say. For example, when the man says 'an intelligent *bein* needs a *doo* share of *appiness*' the words that I've italicised are all items of vocabulary that occur in standard English, but the way they're pronounced (by dropping the 'g' from the end of 'being', writing 'doo' for 'due', and dropping the 'h' from the beginning of 'happiness') indicate a particular non-standard accent. Shaw also represents dialect features, for example, in the phrase 'leave arf the job for me fellow workers'. Here not only does the spelling again indicate the pronunciation of some of the words ('arf' for 'half'), but instead of the standard English possessive adjective 'my', the character uses the non-standard 'me' ('me fellow workers'). When the play is produced on the stage, the actor can supply the accent. But Shaw has made an effort to represent elements of the accent in the written text, possibly as an indicator for actors as to how to interpret the part, and also so that a reading public will be able to construct a mental image of how the man sounds.

## Evaluating language use

All the extracts discussed above are in what are commonly called 'non-standard dialects'. If you look back at how I've described them, I've done so in contrast to a 'standard' English. The idea of standard English is a key concept in sociolinguistics. And one of the key reasons for this is because, when we evaluate different types of language use, we do so with reference to this notion of the standard. Issues about how people evaluate the language use of others are the topic of the reading in the activity below.

### ACTIVITY

The extract below is from an essay called 'Mother tongue' by the Asian-American novelist Amy Tan. Amy Tan was born and brought up in California, and both her parents were immigrants from China. As you'll see, this family background had an influence on the linguistic environment in which she grew up and on her own attitudes to language. While you're reading the essay, think about the following two questions:

1. In what ways do people pre-judge what others say according to the way they say it?

2. How does this type of pre-judging result in a particular type of identity being imposed on Tan's mother?

## READING: Mother tongue

I am not a scholar of English or literature. I cannot give you much more than personal opinions on the English language and its variations in this country or others.

I am a writer. And by that definition, I am someone who has always loved language. I am fascinated by language in daily life. I spend a great deal of my time thinking about the power of language – the way it can evoke an emotion, a visual image, a complex idea, or a simple truth. Language is the tool of my trade. And I use them all – all the Englishes I grew up with.

Recently, I was made keenly aware of the different Englishes I do use. I was giving a talk to a large group of people, the same talk I had already given to half a dozen other groups. The nature of the talk was about my writing, my life, and my book, *The Joy Luck Club*. The talk was going along well enough, until I remembered one major difference that made the whole talk sound wrong. My mother was in the room. And it was perhaps the first time she had heard me give a lengthy speech – using the kind of English I have never used with her. I was saying things like, 'The intersection of memory upon imagination' and 'There is an aspect of my fiction that relates to thus-and-thus' – a speech filled with carefully wrought grammatical phrases, burdened, it suddenly seemed to me, with nominalized forms, past perfect tenses, conditional phrases – all the forms of standard English that I had learned in school and through books, the forms of English I did not use at home with my mother.

Just last week, I was walking down the street with my mother, and I again found myself conscious of the English I was using, the English I do use with her. We were talking about the price of new and used furniture and I heard myself saying this: 'Not waste money that way.' My husband was with us as well, and he didn't notice any switch in my English. And then I realized why. It's because over the twenty years we've been together I've often used that same kind of English with him, and sometimes he even uses it with me. It has become our language of intimacy, a different sort of English that relates to family talk, the language I grew up with.

So you'll have some idea of what this family talk I heard sounds like, I'll quote what my mother said during a recent conversation which I videotaped and then transcribed. During this conversation, my mother was talking about a political gangster in Shanghai who had the same last name as her family's, Du, and how the gangster in his early years wanted to be adopted by her family which was rich by comparison. Later, the gangster became more powerful, far richer than my mother's family, and one day showed up at my mother's wedding to pay his respects. Here's what she said in part:

Du Yusong having business like fruit stand. Like off the street kind. He is Du like Du Zong – but not Tsung-ming Island people. The local people call putong, the river east side, he belong to that side local people. That man want to ask Du Zong father take him in like become own family. Du Zong father wasn't look down on him, but didn't take seriously, until that man big like become a mafia. Now important person, very hard to inviting him. Chinese way, came only to show respect, don't stay for dinner. Respect for making big celebration, he shows up. Mean gives lots of respect. Chinese custom. Chinese social life that way. If too important won't have to stay too long. He come to my wedding. I didn't see, I heard it. I gone to boy's side, they have YMCA dinner. Chinese age I was nineteen.

You should know that my mother's expressive command of English belies how much she actually understands. She reads the Forbes report, listens to Wall Street Week, converses daily with her stockbroker, reads all of Shirley MacLaine's books with ease – all kinds of things I can't begin to understand. Yet some of my friends tell me they understand fifty percent of what my mother says. Some say they understand eighty to ninety percent. Some say they understand none of it, as if she were speaking pure Chinese. But to me, my mother's English is perfectly clear, perfectly natural. It's my mother tongue. Her language, as I hear it, is vivid, direct, full of observation and imagery. That was the language that helped shape the way I saw things, expressed things, made sense of the world.

Lately, I've been giving more thought to the kind of English my mother speaks. Like others, I have described it to people as 'broken' or 'fractured' English. But I wince when I say that. It has always bothered me that I can think of no way to describe it other than 'broken,' as if it were damaged and needed to be fixed, as if it lacked a certain wholeness and soundness. I've heard other terms used, 'limited English,' for example. But they seem just as bad, as if everything is limited, including people's perception of the limited English speaker.

I know this for a fact, because when I was growing up, my mother's 'limited' English limited my perception of her. I was ashamed of her English. I believed that her English reflected the quality of what she had to say. That is, because she expressed them imperfectly her thoughts were imperfect. And I had plenty of empirical evidence to support me: the fact that people in department stores, at banks, and at restaurants did not take her seriously, did not give her good service, pretended not to understand her, or even acted as if they did not hear her.

My mother has long realized the limitations of her English as well. When I was fifteen, she used to have me call people on the phone to pretend I was she. In this guise, I was forced to ask for information or even to complain and yell at people who had been rude to her. One time it was a call to her stockbroker in New York. She had cashed out her small portfolio and it just so happened we were going to go to New York the next week, our very first trip outside California. I had to get on the phone and say in an adolescent voice that was not very convincing, 'This is Mrs. Tan.'

And my mother was standing in the back whispering loudly, 'Why he don't send me check, already two weeks late. So mad he lie to me, losing me money.'

And then I said in perfect English, 'Yes, I'm getting rather concerned. You had agreed to send the check two weeks ago, but it hasn't arrived.'

Then she began to talk more loudly, 'What he want, I come to New York tell him front of his boss, you cheating me?' And I was trying to calm her down, make her be quiet, while telling the stockbroker, 'I can't tolerate any more excuses. If I don't receive the check immediately, I am going to have to speak to your manager when I'm in New York next week.' And sure enough, the following week there we were in front of this astonished stockbroker, and I was sitting there red-faced and quiet, and my mother, the real Mrs. Tan, was shouting at his boss in her impeccable broken English.

(Tan, 1990, pp. 7–8)

## DISCUSSION

As Amy Tan vividly relates, the way that her mother speaks English often gets in the way of what she wants to say. But this isn't because she is unable to express her ideas or wishes; it's because her audience often doesn't listen to the content of her speech because they are put off by the form it takes. She is what is commonly known as a 'non-native speaker'. That is, she learnt the language later in her life, and because of this her accent and use of grammar is strongly influenced by her own native language (Chinese). In the story about the gangster Du, for example, she uses a rather elliptical syntax and strings words together in an ungrammatical way. But, as the essay also observes, her competence in the language – especially in terms of her receptive understanding – is very good. Yet the perception of her communication skills by other people is often prejudiced by the type of English she speaks. People are quick to evaluate what she is saying on the basis of how she is saying it.

Tan's essay was originally presented as a talk as part of a panel entitled 'Englishes: whose English is it anyway?' at the State of the Language Symposium in San Francisco. The title of this panel reflects a debate about English which is attracting a lot of attention around the world at the moment. This is the issue of who *owns* English – that is, does English belong to some people (native English speakers), by virtue of their birth or upbringing, and does this then mean that these people have more right to decide what counts as correct English usage than others do?

At the end of the nineteenth century, Mark Twain asserted that '[t]here is no such thing as the Queen's English. The property has gone into the hands of a joint stock company and we [the United States] own the bulk of the shares' (Twain, 1989 [1897], p. 230). Over a century later, the centre of power has probably shifted even more emphatically towards the USA. Certainly, the population of the USA is far greater than that of the UK, so there is good reason to suggest that standard US English is the dominant model of English in the world today. But another shift has also taken place in the last few decades. English has now come to be a truly global language, and is spoken in areas all around the world. One of the consequences of this global spread is that there are now more users of English who are non-native speakers than those who speak it as their mother tongue. Some estimates suggest that almost 1,500 million people around the world speak English, and only 400 million of these are native speakers (Crystal, 2006, p. 424). In several countries people use English in addition to their native language or languages, and for many other people it is an international form of communication – that is, they use it specifically to talk to people with whom they do not share a mother tongue. In contexts such as these, the form of the language that is used is not necessarily identical to standard British or American English. It may well be something more akin to what Tan's mother speaks. In other words, non-standard forms such as those used by Tan's mother are widespread throughout the world, and in some contexts they are practically the norm. Yet, as we can see from the reading, a common perception is that such forms are failed attempts to speak proper English, and are evaluated as being sub-standard.

Such evaluation does not only occur with respect to non-native English usage though. In the preface to his play *Pygmalion*, Shaw made the satirical assertion that 'it is impossible for an Englishman to open his mouth without making some other Englishman despise him' (1986 [1913], p. 327). He wrote this a century ago, and it might be thought that since then the UK has become less class-conscious and that prejudices based on someone's background are not as widespread as they once were. Up to a point this may well be true, but that is not to say that evaluation about people's way of speaking – and especially their accent and dialect – no longer occurs. In fact, we engage in some form of evaluation of how others speak all the time, even if it is just in terms of spotting a distinctiveness in their manner of speech and associating it with a particular group identity.

As we have seen with the literary examples in the earlier exercises, this notion of identity, and how it is conveyed through speech, is an important one not only in everyday life, but also in the process of creative writing where it can inform the invention and portrayal of different characters. It is this that we will look at in the next chapter.

# 3 Inventing a voice

## Voices and creative writing

In the previous chapter we looked at how speech works in various everyday contexts: how people use language, often very creatively, to communicate with one another. You will also be familiar with speech and conversation in fiction, in plays, in films, in poems and in **life writing**. ('Life writing' is the term used to cover both autobiographical and biographical writing.) In this chapter we will concentrate on prose and drama, and at the creation of characters' voices.

What you first need to recognise about a great deal of creative writing is that voices are, necessarily, representations or approximations of how people actually talk. In prose fiction and drama, the aim is often to create an illusion of reality, to make you feel as if you are eavesdropping on the real thing. At the simplest level, this involves a degree of tidying up how people speak – removing some of the stutters, false starts, hiccups, even confusions that occur when people talk across each other. Speech in fiction and drama is edited.

However, the main aims of speech are to give readers or audiences an insight into the character(s) and the action. Speech in creative writing doesn't have the quality of a transcript – not least because a transcript can be quite dull, and relatively directionless. The invented speech of fiction and drama is necessarily sharper and sometimes more evasive than it might be in 'real life', because the aim is to tell a story. And there is a further complication, too – what works in one genre may not work in another. In Creative Writing, as in Literary Studies, the term **genre** is used in two ways. It literally means (like 'genus' in science), a 'sort' or 'kind'. Creative Writing uses it to distinguish between poetry, drama, fiction and life writing. Each one is a 'genre'. However, 'genre' is often used, a little confusingly, to mean specific kinds of writing within the main genre, such as (in drama) screenplay, stage play, radio play, or (in fiction) crime, horror, romance, science fiction, fantasy, and so on. These divisions are sometimes known instead as 'sub-genres'. It may be the case that what works in the genre of fiction does not work in the genre of drama.

When the novelist and screenwriter Raymond Chandler adapted James M. Cain's *Double Indemnity* (1943) for Billy Wilder's 1944 film, he noted that Cain's dialogue was 'written for the eye not the ear' (MacShane, 1986 [1976], p. 107) – that is, it might work on the page, but it would sound wrong if heard out loud. Chandler rewrote the dialogue so that it suited the film. Or, as we might say, Chandler reinvented the language. In neither Cain's short novel nor in Chandler's script is the language a facsimile of how ordinary people speak. It approximates to it, but it edits and reshapes it. As Robin Cook, a novelist interviewed for Linda Seger's *Creating Unforgettable Characters* (1990), remarks, 'One of the amazing parts of really good dialogue is that it gives you the impression of being in the vernacular without being in the vernacular' (Seger, 1990, p. 168).

This is true even in the case of the British playwright Harold Pinter, whose early work for the stage was much commended for its verisimilitude. It was praised for its use of such devices as pauses (of different length), repetitions and linguistic confusions, as when a character in *A Night Out* (1960) claims that someone is 'very compressed', when he means 'depressed'. Yet Pinter's language was highly stylised. In fact, it's significant that the adjective 'Pinteresque' had made it into the *Oxford English Dictionary* within a few years of his first major stage success. Its definition of the word is 'Of or relating to Harold Pinter; resembling or characteristic of his plays', but adds 'Pinter's plays are typically characterised by implications of threat and strong feeling produced through colloquial language, apparent triviality, and long pauses.' In other words, Pinteresque language resembles the way Pinter writes: it doesn't mean that it is naturalistic. Other playwrights, notably Caryl Churchill, have experimented with overlapping dialogue. Churchill uses a backslash to indicate where speech overlaps, a device that has been widely adopted by other playwrights – but her work is often timed so that characters suddenly speak in unison: we get the 'reality' of people talking across each other, but the speeches are carefully constructed to coincide with and to echo one another. And the American playwright David Mamet, whose *Oleanna* (1993) begins with a telephone conversation, and with a speaker unable to finish his words, and whose trademarks are bursts of unfinished, staccato sentences, which are often described as 'realistic', has said that 'The language in my plays is not realistic but poetic. The words sometimes have a musical quality to them. It's language that is tailor-made for the stage. People don't always talk the way my characters do in real life, although they may use some of the same words ... *It's an illusion*' (Kane, 2001, p. 49; my italics).

## Harold Pinter, Caryl Churchill and David Mamet

Harold Pinter was the author of thirty plays, twenty screenplays and a variety of other writings. He won many awards, including the Nobel Prize for Literature. His first plays were produced in 1957, and his breakthrough came with *The Caretaker* in 1959. Martin Esslin wrote of the 'tape-recorder fidelity' of Pinter's dialogue, and noted that it was, 'superficially at least, of a devastating naturalness … the vocabulary of real conversation … largely missed in stage dialogue that attempted to combine naturalness with good grammar, correct vocabulary and logical progression of its reasoning' (1963, p. 139). Pinter became particularly known for his use of the pause, as here in *The Caretaker*:

DAVIES:   I was saying he's ... he's a bit of a funny bloke, your brother.

   MICK *stares at him.*

MICK:   Funny? Why?

DAVIES:   Well ... he's funny ...

MICK:   What's funny about him?

   *Pause.*

DAVIES:   Not liking work.

MICK:   What's funny about that?

DAVIES:   Nothing.

   *Pause.*

MICK:   I don't call it funny.

DAVIES:   Nor me.

(Pinter, 2006 [1960], pp. 49–50)

Caryl Churchill is a playwright (for radio as well as stage), and has had more than forty plays produced, the most famous of which is *Top Girls* (1982). In her play *Three More Sleepless Nights* (1980), she decided she 'wanted two kinds of quarrel – the one where you can't speak and the one where you both talk at once. When I was writing *Top Girls* I first wrote a draft of the dinner scene with one speech after another and then realised it would be better if the talk overlapped in a similar way. Having got a taste for it I've gone on overlapping in most things I've written since' (Churchill, 1990, p. i). Here are her instructions about the dialogue in one of her other plays, *Fen* (1986):

A speech usually follows the one immediately before it BUT:

1. When one character starts speaking before the other has finished, the point of interruption is marked /.

    e.g. DEB:   You shut up, / none of your business.
    
      MAY:   Don't speak to your mum like that  etc.

2. A character sometimes continues speaking right through another's speech:

    e.g. GEOFFREY:      We had terrible times. If I had cracked tomatoes for my tea / I
    
      SHIRLEY:      It's easy living here like I do now.
      
      GEOFFREY:      thought I was lucky. etc.

(Churchill, 1986, pp. 53–4)

David Mamet is an American playwright and screenwriter, as well as a film director and critic. He has written more than twenty plays, and, including adaptations of his own stage plays, over twenty films. Among his best-known works are *Glengarry Glen Ross* (1992) and *Oleanna*. His characters often speak in a staccato, half-finished fashion, as in this extract from *Oleanna*:

JOHN:      (*Picks up paper.*) Here: Please: Sit down. (*Pause*) Sit down. (*Reads from her paper.*) 'I think that the ideas contained in this work express the author's feelings in a way that he intended, based on his results.' What can that mean? Do you see? What ...

CAROL:      I, the best that I ...

JOHN:      I'm saying, that perhaps this course ...

CAROL:      No, no, no, you can't, you can't ... I have to ...

JOHN:      ... how ...

CAROL:      ... I have to pass it ...

JOHN:      Carol, I:

CAROL:      I *have* to pass this course, I ...

JOHN:      Well.

(Mamet, 1993, pp. 8–9)

In the next activity, you will look at how people actually speak in real life by reading an extract from a transcript of the 'Watergate' tapes. These were recordings made of conversations in the Oval Office of the White House. The speaker here, H.R. 'Bob' Haldeman, is talking to the Republican president, Richard Nixon, about a break-in at the Watergate Hotel, the headquarters of the Democratic Party, during the 1972 election campaign. Haldeman was Nixon's chief of staff, and, like other aides, was unaware that all conversations were being recorded. The recordings later led to Nixon's resignation.

## ACTIVITY

Read the following extract from the transcript. As you read, think about why Haldeman's speech would fail to work in a play or a piece of prose fiction.

HALDEMAN: Okay – that's fine. Now, on the investigation, you know, the Democratic break-in thing, we're back to the – in the, the problem area because the FBI is not under control, because Gray doesn't exactly know how to control them, and they have, their investigation is now leading into some productive areas, because they've been able to trace the money, not through the money itself, but through the bank, you know, sources – the banker himself. And, and it goes in some directions we don't want it to go. Ah, also there have been some things, like an informant came in off the street to the FBI in Miami, who was a photographer or has a friend who is a photographer who developed some films through this guy, Barker, and the films had pictures of Democratic National Committee letter head documents and things. So I guess, so it's things like that that are gonna, that are filtering in. Mitchell came up with yesterday, and John Dean analyzed very carefully last night and concludes, concurs now with Mitchell's recommendation that the only way to solve this, and we're set up beautifully to do it, ah, in that and that … the only network that paid any attention to it last night was NBC … they did a massive story on the Cuban …

PRESIDENT: That's right.

HALDEMAN: thing.

PRESIDENT: Right.

(Nixon and Haldeman, 1999–2002 [1972])

## DISCUSSION

You have probably spotted that the speech here is too rambling to hold a reader's attention. Almost at its outset, there is a complex sentence that piles up clauses, and alters the grammar as it goes along:

> Now, on the investigation, you know, the Democratic break-in thing, we're back to the – in the, the problem area because the FBI is not under control, because Gray doesn't exactly know how to control them, and they have, their investigation is now leading into some productive areas, because they've been able to trace the money, not through the money itself, but through the bank, you know, sources – the banker himself.

Even if I tell you what you might guess (that Gray is head of the FBI), you would, I suspect, have trouble understanding 'we're back to the – in the, the problem area' and 'they've been able to trace the money, not through the money itself, but through the bank, you know, sources – the banker himself' and 'So I guess, so it's things like that that are gonna, that are filtering in.'

For the purpose of a play or piece of prose fiction, accuracy or fidelity to everyday speech is not the issue. We can tell that Haldeman is struggling with his thoughts, and he is after all addressing the President, so a degree of extra hesitation might be unsurprising. But fictional characters, created characters, have to communicate information not only to another character but also to an audience, and they may well have to communicate information about the story in which they 'exist'. If you were to dramatise or to fictionalise Haldeman's speech here, you would want not only to show him as anxious and uncertain, but also to make much clearer what he is talking about. That would mean, at the least, trimming away much of what he says, reducing his rambling. He is trying to suggest that the head of the FBI is not in control of events, and that this is potentially damaging to the president's authority. Perhaps he might be made to say

> The problem … the problem is that Gray can't control the FBI. They're finding out about the sources of the money. And that – that could mean – that could be difficult. For us. It could be very difficult.

This is a great deal more coherent than what was actually said, although notice that it uses some pauses, some repetitions and some hesitations. These are included to suggest the anxiety. They are also intended to mimic or to give the impression of some aspects of every-day speech: enough to convince a reader or a listener. My edit has also reduced the length of the speech. While it is perfectly possible for there to be lengthy passages of speech in drama or prose narrative, most speech is relatively short. This is because writing depends for the most part on being active, on possessing forward movement.

# Distinguishing one voice from another

Voices are crucial to writers, because voices mark characters out, and characters are at the heart of almost every good story. Nothing is more undramatic – or confusing – than having all the characters speak in exactly the same way. If you are watching a play or film you can see who is speaking, of course, but it would still be tedious if everyone spoke in the same fashion: as we discussed in the previous chapter, the way people express themselves is the key to their identity.

When we make someone speak in a drama or prose fiction, we may of course be leading, or misleading, the reader as to what direction the story will take. The voice we provide may offer up facts, whole, partial or illusory, and this contributes to the overall narrative. But for the moment, I would like you to concentrate on the process of creating a character through voice.

---

## ACTIVITY

Suppose you are writing a story, in any medium or genre, and your character is explaining that he or she is late for an appointment or an event. Think of a few ways in which the character might admit to being late, and see if you can make what they say tell us something about their character and identity. One or two sentences for each character are all you need to create. When you have finished, have a look at my suggestions.

## DISCUSSION

Here are five possibilities:

1. Late again, that's me!

2. This watch has let me down all week: it's useless.

3. Please may I apologise profusely for my tardiness. Inexcusable of me.

4. How come it's always you that's on time, and never me?

5. Okay, so I'm late. So what?

As we saw in the activity on different ways to say 'thank-you' in the previous chapter, each of these conveys a different impression. The speaker in Example 1 sounds like a bubbly, unapologetic, maybe even a slightly ditsy individual – an outgoing, happy-go-lucky type. In Example 2 the speaker sounds impatient, disagreeable and ready to blame anyone or anything rather than apologise.

The speaker in Example 3 is formal: in fact, absurdly formal, perhaps pompous. (He might also be the kind of person who says 'Thanks awfully', in the earlier activity.) In Example 4, the speaker is probably an ironist, the kind of person who likes to make a joke out of life. And the speaker in Example 5 seems blunt, to the point of rudeness.

Of course, the context in which the examples were spoken, or the intonation of the speakers, might change the way in which we interpret each of those lines. If the character habitually came out with these kinds of remark, though, we would begin to learn what to expect. (Remember however that, if these were the first encounters with the characters, the expectation might later be reversed.)

---

In the above examples, what matters is not the information that the character is late but the implied attitude of the speaker. This is because creative writing is nearly always concerned with building up character by indirect means: this is what allows readers and audiences to engage with the character and the story itself. There is no intrigue if a character arrives and announces 'I'm pompous' (which a pompous character is not likely to do). A pompous voice needs to be established by the way it uses language, just as pompous characters need to be established by the actions they undertake. Equally important is what is not said, not undertaken.

---

## ACTIVITY

Try the previous activity again, this time choosing a different subject and producing four examples of ways of making a statement, request or announcement about the same thing. You may choose any subject you like, but here are some suggestions your character might be doing:

1. complimenting someone on their appearance

2. asking someone else to lend them some money

3. making a marriage proposal.

## DISCUSSION

It might be helpful to test the lines on a friend, to see whether you have achieved the effect you hope for. You can do this in two ways – show them the remark on a piece of paper or read it out to them. It is best to let someone see or hear the different 'voices' one at a time (remember that reading them out loud will be hard to do without adding some idea of what you intended, because you are likely to add intonation). The trick is to have the voices contrasting with one another – and this is a topic we'll return to in Chapter 5.

## The narrator's voice

In fiction and in life writing, stories are told. It is not merely the voices of the people in a story that engage a reader. When writing a story, you have to consider the narrative point of view from which the story is being told, and there are many different ways of intriguing a reader, depending on your strategy. You might use quite a neutral narrative voice, in which case the significance of voice passes to a greater degree to the characters. But equally you might tell the story from the point of view of one of the characters - someone who is directly involved in the action or on its periphery. peripheral **narrator** is sometimes called a 'witness narrator' - one of the most famous being Nick Carraway in F. Scott Fitzgerald's novel *The Great Gatsby* (1925), who observes the actions of the other characters, but does not take a central part in the action.

Having a character tell the story is not at all unusual. Many pieces of fiction, and almost all autobiographical life writing, are told in the first person. The voice you give this first-person narrator is important, not least because it is likely to be biased or opinionated. First-person narrators may even be made 'unreliable', i.e. we can't trust what they tell us: this is a device many creative writers have used in order to create tension in a story, forcing the reader to assess and reassess their own responses. Famous instances of this are Ford Madox Ford's *The Good Soldier* (1915), Henry James's *The Turn of the Screw* (1898), Kazuo Ishiguro's *The Remains of the Day* (1989), and Jane Gardam's *The Queen of the Tambourine* (1992).

### ACTIVITY

Here is the opening passage of *Tono-Bungay* (1909) by H.G. Wells. It is narrated by the central character, George Ponderevo. What do you make of Ponderevo, judging by his voice? Think about the tone of the voice, and also its rhythm.

> I have got an unusual series of impressions that I want very urgently to tell. I have seen life at very different levels, and at all these levels I have seen it with a sort of intimacy and in good faith. I have been a native in many social countries. I have been the unwelcome guest of a working baker, my cousin, who has since died in the Chatham infirmary; I have eaten illegal snacks – the unjustifiable gifts of

footmen – in pantries, and been despised for my want of style (and subsequently married and divorced) by the daughter of a gasworks clerk; and – to go to my other extreme – I was once – oh, glittering days! – an item in the house-party of a countess. She was, I admit, a countess with a financial aspect, but still, you know, a countess. I've seen these people at various angles. At the dinner-table I've met not simply the titled but the great. On one occasion – it is my brightest memory – I upset my champagne over the trousers of the greatest statesman in the empire – Heaven forbid I should be so invidious as to name him! – in the warmth of our mutual admiration.

And once (though it is the most incidental thing in my life) I murdered a man …

(Wells, 2005 [1909], pp. 9–10)

## DISCUSSION

You may have sensed that this is a narrator in a hurry, a character from whom words spill with prodigal speed. The way the speaker switches subjects so rapidly, and interrupts himself with asides, such as 'oh, glittering days!' and 'it is my brightest memory', combine to suggest someone who is intense, upbeat, on the verge of being boastful. Perhaps you might think this egotistical strain in the voice is mitigated by a sense of impish, candid glee. Wells also enjoys teasing the reader – there is something quite calculated about Ponderevo's chatter, not least in the way he refers, mock-casually, to murder as 'incidental' in the last, elliptical line. And the rhythm is driven, energetic, hectic, as if the narrator is something of a gas-bag. Importantly for a fictional voice, he makes you want to read on, and follow him as 'urgently' as he says he is explaining himself. It has the patter, I would say, of a spoken voice: a sort of intimacy, although deliberately coy.

## ACTIVITY

Now see if you can write 100–200 words of 'voice' that create a character. Remember, it is important not to be direct about the character's qualities – these should be implied by the way the character speaks.

## DISCUSSION

You will probably find this activity easier to achieve if you do not start with a set idea in your mind. It is best to think of a situation in which to place your character, and to see how the character develops. Although creative writing entails forward planning, the early stages – finding voices, finding characters – is best achieved by discovering the voice or character as you go, and editing what you have done afterwards.

## Varying the voice

Something else you need to consider, unless you have a very good reason to do otherwise, is varying the pattern of an individual's speech. This is true of **monologue** or protracted speech in a play, and also of a narrator, or indeed a character in fiction. Here is an invented example of an unvarying voice:

> The day after that, I was miserable. My feet dragged along the local road. I found that I was nearly tearful. The prospect of fresh air didn't thrill. The clouds inhabited the sky like hermits. What made others smile remained a mystery. Sounds of distant children left me cold. Any stranger passing me received no greeting. I was interested only in my grief. My morning meal lay leaden inside me. Nothing seemed to shake me from torpor.

I could go on, but the likelihood is that you too would fall into a torpor or even a coma. I think the point has been made – told rather than shown, notice, too – but the rhythm is utterly flat, unrelieved. And the reason for that is that I have put seven words in every sentence. Even if I wanted to create a monotonous voice (and I suspect I have!), I have committed the cardinal sin here of boring the audience. Here is a (true) story from my childhood: I hope you'll see that the length of the sentences is varied.

> I buried my brother just to the right of the garage, which housed my father's very fast car. He was addicted to speed (the first book I remember reading was *Speed Was My Life* by Alfred Neubauer, the team manager of Mercedes. My father only ever read sports books, or James Bond novels), and had an E-type Jaguar, one of the first. I hated it, because of the odour of fresh leather, and my allergic reaction to movement of any sort. I wasn't born to move about too much. I was a bookworm instead, and burrowed my way through all ten volumes of *Newnes Pictorial Encyclopedia*, on which my world-view is still probably very dependent. Once I had bored my way through this pile of knowledge, I bored my way through everyone who came into contact with me, too. Facts and more facts. I was able to recite them like a parakeet on a power-surge.
>
> My brother's grave was not peculiarly elaborate. The soil was moist, and the spade I used, although it was too big for me, did the job easily. It was shallow enough to rest a length of corrugated iron over a four-year-old, and easy enough to disguise the iron with further spadefuls of earth, until there was a satisfying mound, at the end of which I planted a rough cross, with a plastic helmet resting on it at an angle. To be fair, my brother had not objected to being buried. After all, I had supplied him with a) a flashlight, b) a comic, and c) a length of hose from his underground resting-place

to the open air above. I thought my mother would be impressed with my handiwork, and did some shouting at her.

'I'm busy, Bill,' she said through the kitchen window.

'But I want you to see. It will only take a tick.'

After some persuasion, she came to see what I had been up to. It was probably out of some misplaced relief that I wasn't buried in a book.

She inspected the graveyard, and nodded some bewildered approbation. At this point my brother piped up with 'Hello Mummy!' She seemed quite indignant at my initial reluctance to dig him up.

It's my voice, but I am manipulating it, to make sure that you are more engaged with the more disturbing elements of my eight-year-old psyche. Partly I've done this by digression, but also through some repetition of key words, to connect the sentences together (perhaps most ostentatiously by referring to being 'buried' in a book). The punctuation is important, too: breaking the pattern of the sentences up. There are longer sentences jostling with shorter ones (at one point, a fifty-two-word sentence followed by an eleven-word sentence). Variety in voice necessitates variety of pace.

In this chapter, I hope we've identified even more clearly what we said in the Introduction. A knowledge of what we mean by 'language' is important to how we operate together in society, to how we see ourselves, and to how we see others. But when we come to represent that language creatively for the purpose of exploring ideas and characters, in telling a story, we adapt the language. The words we use in everyday language are arranged, composed, edited, using a process of fabrication. 'The function of selection and arrangement is mine,' as Harold Pinter said of his writing. 'I do all the donkeywork' (Pinter, 1991, p. xiii). As a writer, you have to take the everyday language and place it in a new structure, a new context. To understand how to fictionalise and dramatise the language of the 'real world', you need to know how that real world is using language every day, and how people perceive and evaluate the speech of others. It is this that we turn to in the next chapter, where we look especially at the notion of 'standard English'.

# 4    Speech and conversation

## Standard language

At the beginning of her essay 'Mother Tongue', Amy Tan talked about 'the forms of standard English that I had learned in school and through books'. It is this idea of the standard that is often key to the way that people's use of English is evaluated. It is standard English that acts as a benchmark against which other usages are compared – and often judged. Both regional dialects and social dialects are defined in contrast to the notion of a standard. As such, it is worth investigating what people mean by the term, and where the concept came from. As we shall see, it is not quite as straight-forward as it might seem.

Let's begin this chapter by looking at an extract from a book called *English with an Accent* by Rosina Lippi-Green. In this reading, Lippi-Green discusses some definitions of a standard language, and points to a number of problems in the way these definitions conceive of the concept. She is writing specifically about standard US English, and is concentrating mostly on pronunciation (and thus accent). But the issues she raises are the same for any other standard English (e.g. standard British English), and can also apply to dialect.

---

### ACTIVITY

Before looking at the reading, take a couple of minutes to jot down a few notes about what the term 'standard English' suggests to you. Do you think that the concept of a standard language is important, and if so why? Where do you think the standard language comes from, and how is it maintained?

Now look at the extract from *English with an Accent*. As you read, think about the following questions:

1. According to the definitions Lippi-Green analyses, what or who provides the model for standard English?

2. What does she mean when she says that standard English is determined by those who have authority?

3. Why does she liken standard English to certain 'mythical, imaginary constructs'?

---

### READING: What we call standard US English

People are quite comfortable with the idea of a standard language, so much so that they have no trouble describing and defining it, much in the same way that most people could draw a unicorn, or describe a being from *Star Trek*'s planet Vulcan, or tell us who King Arthur was and why he needed a Round Table. For the most part these definitions will be firmly founded in the understanding that these are mythical, imaginary constructions; nevertheless, the definitions will have much in common, because they are part of our shared cultural heritage.

The way we conceive and define standard US English brings to light a number of assumptions and misassumptions about language. *Merriam-Webster's Collegiate Dictionary* (tenth edition, 1993), which proclaims itself *The Voice of Authority*, provides a typical definition:

> Standard English: the English that with respect to spelling, grammar, pronunciation, and vocabulary is substantially uniform though not devoid of regional differences, that is well established by usage in the formal and informal speech and writing of the educated, and that is widely recognized as acceptable wherever English is spoken and understood.

This definition assumes that the written and spoken language are equal, in terms of both how they are used, and how they should be used. It sets spelling and pronunciation on a common footing, and compounds this generalization by bringing in both formal and informal language use. While the definition makes some room for 'regional differences' it makes none at all for social ones, and in fact it is quite definite about the social construction of standard US English: it is the language of the educated. What is meant by 'educated' is left unstated in this entry, and its implications are not fully explored anywhere else in the dictionary. What language might be spoken by those who are the *opposite* of the educated is also not made clear, but whoever these people are, they are drawn into the definition by its final component: standard US English is *acceptable wherever English is spoken and understood*. The lexicographer assumes the consent of the non-educated, uneducated, or lesser educated to the authority of the educated in matters of written and spoken language.

Other definitions bring some important generalizations about standard US English to the fore: *Cambridge International Dictionary of English* (first edition, 1995) also cites educated speakers as the sole possessors of the standard language, but they bring in a specific subgroup of the educated in that they assert that 'most announcers on the BBC speak standard English.' *Chambers Dictionary* (1994) is more specific about the path to standard US English: 'the form of English taught in schools.' In 1978 the *English Journal* noted a general perception in the public of a '"standard standard". Some people call it "broadcast" or "publications" standard, because most newspapers and television news shows use it.'

More specific information on exactly how the lexicographer draws on the language of the educated is provided by interviews with the pronunciation editor at Merriam-Webster which appeared in various newspapers around the appearance of that dictionary's tenth edition. It falls to the pronunciation editor to decide which possible pronunciations are included in the dictionary, and how they are ordered. 'Usage dictates acceptability,' he is reported as saying. 'There is no other non-arbitrary way to decide' (*New York Times*, July 22, 1993: C1, C8).

In order to pin down this 'majority rule' the editor listens to 'talk shows, medical shows, interviews, news, commentary, the weather' (ibid.) on the radio and on television. The editorial preface to the dictionary is more specific about this procedure; it lists politicians, professors, curators, artists, musicians, doctors, engineers, preachers, activists, and journalists among the type of educated person whose English is consulted as a part of this process.

> In truth, though, there can be no objective standard for correct pronunciation other than the usage of thoughtful and, in particular, educated speakers of English. Among such speakers one hears much variation in pronunciation ... [our attempt is to] include all variants of a word that are used by educated speakers.
> (*Merriam-Webster's Collegiate Dictionary*, tenth edition, 1993: 31a)

The editors claim an objective standard (that of the language of the educated) and at the same time they acknowledge variation among educated speakers. This apparent inconsistency is resolved by the policy which includes *all variants that are used by educated speakers*. A close look at the pronunciations listed in the dictionary, however, indicates that this cannot be the case. An entry with three or more possible pronunciations is rare. If Merriam-Webster's *Dictionary* truly intends to include all pronunciations of the educated, then their definition of who is educated must be very narrow.

It must be clear that this process cannot be representative in any real way. What proportion of even the *educated* population has regular access to the broadcast media? How many of us discuss our views on the budget, on foreign affairs, or on local government in a forum which is broadcast to a wider audience? The *uneducated*, who by the dictionary definition must constitute the greatest number of native speakers of English, are even less represented.

Perhaps there is no way to write a dictionary which is truly descriptive in terms of pronunciation; perhaps it is necessary to choose one social group to serve as a model. Perhaps there is even some rationale for using the 'educated' as this group. But there is nothing *objective* about this practice. It is the ordering of social groups in terms of who has authority to determine how language is *best used*.

(Lippi-Green, 1997, pp. 53–5)

## DISCUSSION

The central argument that Rosina Lippi-Green puts forward is that the type of English promoted by dictionaries as being the model for 'standard English' is a usage originally associated with one particular section of society. The dictionaries she looks at all state that the usage they're describing is that of 'educated' native speakers. But when we start examining what this means in practice, the issue becomes rather complicated. Who exactly counts as an 'educated' speaker? Does someone have to be educated to a particular level, or have gone to a particular school or college, or be part of a particular profession? Her conclusion is that there is no way in which a dictionary can be an *objective* description of standard pronunciation of the language. Instead, this standard is modelled on the usage patterns (the dialect and accent) of a particular social group. And the reason that this group rather than another gets to provide the model for standard English is because the group has a position of power and influence in society. It thus has the authority to impose its norms on society and to promote them as standard. For this reason she likens the concept of standard English to 'mythical, imaginary constructions' such as unicorns and King Arthur. Standard English is an idea that many people believe in, but if taken too literally it belies the variety and diversity of the way people actually use the language.

If the idea of a standard English is in some ways an idealisation, how then has it come about? Has the notion always existed? Or was there a time when people didn't view variety as problematic, and didn't see some types of usage as more 'correct' than others?

In the next reading the British linguist David Crystal writes about the history of standard English and how it developed in the British Isles. His focus in this passage is on the period of Middle English – that is, the form the language took between the Norman Conquest and the beginning of the Renaissance (i.e. in the period from about 1100 to 1500).

## ACTIVITY

As you read the extract below, note the different ways Crystal suggests that a standard can be established, and how it happened in the case of English. What role is played by authority in the emergence of a standard?

## READING: The emerging standard

Standard languages arise in many ways. They can evolve over a long period of time associated with a particular body of religious or literary writing. Or an official body can be created (an Academy) which 'institutionalizes' a language by organizing the compilation of dictionaries, grammars, and manuals of style. In a further scenario, a standard can arrive, quite literally, overnight: a government selects a dialect of a language, prepares its people, and on a certain legally defined day it becomes the medium of national communication. Sometimes, more than one dialect is selected as the basis of the standard, and a planned amalgamation of forms takes place, as happened to Romansh in Switzerland in the 1980s when Rumantsch Grischun was devised, based on a collation of forms from the major dialects. It is even possible for a country to have two standard varieties of a language, as in the case of Norway, where Bokmål and Nynorsk have been in official coexistence since 1884.

In England, at the end of the Middle Ages, a standard language began to emerge, but it was in no way planned or institutionalized. There was no government intervention. No official bodies were established – the age predated the arrival of Academies in Europe (the first such body, in Italy, was not established until 1582). There were no pundits arguing for a policy of standardization. There was not even a long-standing body of comprehensible English classical literature to look back to: Old English was a foreign language to most people by then, as William Caxton observed in his Preface to *Eneydos* (c. 1490):

> And also my lorde Abbot of Westmynster ded [did] do shewe to me late certayn evydences wryton in olde Englysshe for to reduce it into our Engylysshe now usid. And certaynly it was wreton in suche wyse that it was more lyke to Dutche than Englysshe: I coude not reduce ne [nor] brynge it to be understonden.

In 1400 Chaucer's writing had yet to achieve classical status, and English translation of the Bible had hardly begun, notwithstanding Wycliffe's pioneering role in the 1380s. At the beginning of the fifteenth century, anyone who might have reflected on the need for a standard English language would have found it difficult to see where it could possibly come from. Yet, by the end of the century, its basis was definitely there.

It is difficult to resist the conclusion that Standard English, like Harriet Beecher Stowe's Topsy, 'just growed' – largely unselfconsciously during the fifteenth century, and increasingly self-aware thereafter. The growth took a long time – some 300 years, indeed, before the phenomenon, as we recognize it today, was firmly established. It is important to reiterate: only the *basis* of Standard English existed by 1500. Comparing the kind of language which was being written and spoken in those days to the kind of language we associate with Standard English now, we see a wide range of differences. The clear-cut distinction between 'correct' and 'incorrect' did not exist in late Middle English – that was an eighteenth-century development. There was much greater flexibility over the range of forms which educated people were able to use. And a great deal of variation, a legacy of earlier Middle English, was still in evidence. Apart from anything else, the language was still experiencing the consequences of the period of radical grammatical change which had begun at the end of the Old English period. In the fifteenth century it was undergoing a major shift in pronunciation norms. And its lexicon was continuing to grow rapidly through the introduction of large numbers of loanwords. A standard language presupposes a certain amount of stability: people have to be using the same set of rules, enabling them to distinguish between what is 'right' and what is 'wrong'. It would take a while before these judgements would be made with the kind of arrogant confidence which later became routine.

(Crystal, 2005, pp. 222–3)

## DISCUSSION

Many of the ways Crystal suggests that a standard language can be established relate directly to the execution of authority by powerful institutions. Governments can select which dialect will be used as a standard, and then promote this via dictionaries and grammar books. Or the standard can evolve based on an influential literary tradition – and in this way standard languages are related to the establishments of literary canons. In the case of English, however, standardisation came about without the direct intervention of a single powerful institution. It was a more 'organic' process, the result of the influence of the publishing industry, of literary writers and scholars, of scientific institutions, of influential political and public figures, all combining over the years to promote one variety of the language over others. It was, nevertheless, a historical process. In the fourteenth century there was no real concept of standard English at all. By the eighteenth century the notion as we know it today had become fully formed.

Viewed from this perspective, standard English can be seen as a 'historical construct' rather than a naturally occurring phenomenon – that is, there is nothing inevitable or inviolable about standard English. If the history of the UK had been different, the nature of standard British English would very likely be different as well. Now that it has become established in society, however, it acts as a **prestige variety**, and in many contexts is seen as the most appropriate form of the language to use, at least in a majority of formal or public settings. In other words, it does now exist, for good or for bad, as the benchmark against which judgements about what is 'right' and what is 'wrong' are regularly made. And as we discussed in Chapter 2, these types of judgements play a role in the way people interpret the identity and attitude of other people.

## Drawing on different dialects and languages

In her essay, Amy Tan also wrote of the way that she shifted between two different styles of English when talking to different people. She says she was doing this almost without registering it, and it was only when her mother was in the audience for her talk at the university – that is, when two different domains of her life came together – that she became self-conscious about the different 'Englishes' that she was regularly speaking. In this particular example, Tan was drawing attention to the fact that she used different styles of speech for different contexts. In Chapter 6 we'll explore this idea in greater detail with reference to the way that different domains of life often require different types of language use. For the moment, though, I want to look at a related issue: how people draw on different accents, dialects and languages as part of the communicative process, and how the use of 'mixed' styles indicates something about someone's personal and cultural history.

Throughout the book so far we have been discussing ways in which how a person says something can be as meaningful as what he or she says, and we have noted that this is often related to the fact that the form of language people use is closely tied to their identity. Identity, though, is a complex issue. People rarely, if ever, fit into easily definable boxes. Everyone's personal biography and family history is different, and this unique background will contribute to who they are as an individual. This background will also have an influence on the way they speak, so that their language will have traces of the various different elements that combine to produce their identities. And this is true not just for individual people, but for groups within society as well.

To explore this issue, let's look at a short exchange from *The Island* by Athol Fugard, John Kani, and Winston Ntshona, which is a play about political prisoners on Robben Island in South Africa (where Nelson Mandela was imprisoned) during the apartheid era. The play is written in English, but uses occasional words from other languages.

---

## ACTIVITY

The two characters in the extract below – John and Winston – are both black South Africans who have been imprisoned in very harsh conditions for their political activities. They are talking about how to deal with the brutal prison guard, Hodoshe (this is his nickname). The 'beach' they refer to in the last line is where they do hard labour each day, breaking and carrying rocks in the blazing sun. Read through the dialogue and note the words and phrases that are not in English. Why do you think that there are a number of foreign words in what is otherwise an English-language dialogue?

| | |
|---|---|
| JOHN: | You know what I'm saying? |
| WINSTON: | *Ja.* |
| JOHN: | What? |
| WINSTON: | What 'What'? |
| JOHN: | What am I saying? |
| WINSTON: | *Haai*, Johnny, man! I'm tired now! Let a man … |

JOHN: I'm saying Don't be Hard-Arsed! You! When Hodoshe opens that door tomorrow say, '*Ja, Baas*' the right way. I don't want to be back on that bloody beach tomorrow just because you feel like being difficult.

(Fugard, 1993, p. 20)

## DISCUSSION

In this short exchange three different languages are being used. The main one is English. But in addition there are a few words in both Afrikaans ('*Ja, Baas*') and Xhosa ('*Haai*', '*Hodoshe*').

South Africa is a decidedly multilingual society, and the country presently has eleven **official languages**. (An 'official language' is one which has a special legal status in a country, and is used in contexts such as administration and education.) During apartheid, there were only two official languages: English and Afrikaans. In 1994, after the end of apartheid, the new constitution gave official status to eleven languages: English, Afrikaans and nine indigenous African.

Due to this multilingual context, it isn't odd that the characters should use a mix of different languages. They are not, after all, 'foreign' languages for the society as a whole. They are all part of the general linguistic make-up of South Africa as a nation. But they are also languages that have different histories within the country, and thus have different associations for different sections of the population. Afrikaans is the language that developed from the Dutch spoken by the colonising powers in the seventeenth century. In this exchange, John switches into Afrikaans when discussing what Winston should say to the prison guard: '*Ja, Baas*' ('Yes, boss'). In the context in which it is used here, Afrikaans appears to be a language related to institutional power – the characters use it when interacting with the authority figure in the play – and this may be a reflection of the language's colonial heritage. Xhosa, on the other hand, is a Bantu language that was spoken in the region before the colonial period. It is also the language originally spoken by Nelson Mandela's family. In this section of dialogue the characters use it on two occasions. Winston cries out '*Haai*' (a general exclamation of surprise or alarm), and it is used for the nickname they have for the chief warder, 'Hodoshe' (meaning 'carrion fly'). So Xhosa appears to be used here for more personal meanings: for the expression of emotions, and for the private nicknames they have for the figure of authority.

What we can see from this example is that not only does the mixing of several languages reflect the multilingual nature of the society, but that the choice of which language to use when is related to the history of the society and to the identity of the people involved in the discussion. The switch from one language to another is not random. Instead, the language in which different expressions are made is significant because of the associations that that language has in that society and for those particular characters. So the choice of which language to say something in is itself meaningful, and expresses aspects of people's relationships with each other.

## The structure of conversation

Another important way in which *how* we speak is influenced by social norms is in the act of conversation itself. Just as all dialects, including 'non-standard' ones, have regular rules, so the act of conversation also conforms to very specific patterns. And although we may not be conscious of these patterns when we are talking, they organise the way we interact with each other and provide a structure for all our conversations.

The study of how people converse is known as **conversation analysis**, and was first developed by the sociologists Harvey Sacks, Emanuel Schegloff and Gail Jefferson (1974). They examined in detail what it is that people do when they are engaged in conversation, and how transitions from one speaker to another occur. What they found is that even in the most casual conversations, people conform to a number of specific conventions which structure their interaction. And although many of the observations about these structures may, on the surface, seem rather obvious and lacking in insight, taken together they create a robust picture of how conversations 'work'.

A first observation about the organising principles behind conversations is that people don't generally speak at the same time as each other. Instead, they take turns. There are certain situations where overlapping talk does occur: such as competitive talk, when each of the participants is vying to take centre stage; and collaborative talk, where the overlapping speech indicates that people are following each other's utterances very closely. But on the whole, conversation alternates from speaker to speaker very smoothly. A related observation is that people don't leave gaps as the conversation switches from one speaker to another. As soon as one speaker completes an utterance, the interlocutor usually picks up the conversation almost immediately.

Based on these two observations, a key question that conversation analysis asks is how people signal to each other that a transition can occur. That's to say, what mechanisms exist that allow people to co-ordinate their turn-taking successfully. And an important part of the answer to this question is that some kinds of turn typically follow others, and that this creates expectations that structure the interaction. We can illustrate this with the activity below.

## ACTIVITY

Have a look at the following three utterances. What type of response would you expect each of them to elicit?

1. Morning!

2. Do you know who first coined the phrase 'Six Degrees of Separation'?

3. Would you like to go out to dinner sometime; maybe next Thursday?

## DISCUSSION

For each of these examples, the form that the expected response will take seems pretty obvious. Example 1 is a greeting, and so a typical response would be a reciprocal greeting. Example 2 is a query, and thus we'd expect an answer in response (e.g. 'No, I'm afraid I have no idea. Why don't you try looking it up on Wikipedia?'). And Example 3 is an invitation, which typically calls either for an acceptance or rejection (e.g. 'Sorry, I'm visiting my uncle in Albuquerque all next week').

Each of the above are what are known as **adjacency pairs**, and they provide a regular pattern for conversational interactions. What's of particular interest is exactly how these patterns are used in real-life situations to generate meaning between participants. After all, just because the expectation is that a greeting will be followed by a greeting or that an invitation will elicit an acceptance or rejection, this doesn't mean they always necessarily do. Consider, for example, the following three answers to the above questions. If you were to receive these as responses, what would you infer about what your interlocutor was trying to communicate?

1. – Morning!
   – Yes, I did exactly the same thing.

2. – Do you know who first coined the phrase 'Six Degrees of Separation'?
   – Do you know who first coined the phrase 'I couldn't care less'?

3. – Would you like to go out to dinner sometime; maybe next Thursday?
   – [Two-second pause] Well, I think I might, um ... Do you mind if I close the window? It's a bit cold in here.

Failure to respond to a greeting with a reciprocal greeting, as is happening in Example 1, could mean a number of things. In this particular instance the most likely inference is probably that the interlocutor has simply misheard the original greeting, and is responding to a different utterance altogether. Other reasons for failing to respond with a reciprocal greeting could be that the interlocutor wants to dispense with any pleasantries and get straight down to business. In either instance, breaking the expected pattern is, in itself, a form of communication.

Likewise in Example 2, the meaning of the response comes as much from the context in which it is given as the content of the words. Rather than respond with an answer to the question, the interlocutor replies with a question of her own. In this way she subverts the intentions of the first speaker, and signals a dismissive attitude to the original question (the fact that her own question mocks the form of the original question adds, of course, to the flippant attitude).

For those adjacency pairs where there are two possible responses – such as acceptance/rejection or agreement/disagreement – analysts talk of 'preferred' and 'dispreferred' responses. A preferred response is what the person asking the question or giving the invitation is expecting or hoping to receive. In the case of the original question in Example 3, this would be a positive reply to the invitation to go out. Preferred responses are typically made very quickly, without any pause between the turns. Dispreferred responses, on the other hand, are those which run counter to what is expected or sought, and these are often marked by a delay, as is the case in Example 3. The very act of pausing too long before the response can indicate that the respondent is not going to accept the invitation.

As we can see, then, the structured nature of conversations means that not only are people able to organise their social interaction according to shared conventions, but a great deal can be expressed simply through the manipulation of these structures. In addition, we are able to make judgements about people's personality based on the way they manage the turn-taking in a conversation. For example, someone who dominates the conversation by refusing to leave pauses for others to come in on, avoids eye-contact and begins raising his voice when others are trying to interject, is expressing a sense of arrogance – and doing so through the style rather than the substance of his conversation. An analysis of how people cooperate with each other in the negotiation of the conversation can therefore be used to gauge a lot about characteristics such as politeness, brusqueness, self-importance and so on, as well as whether the speaker is in a position of power or lacks self-confidence.

Throughout both this chapter and Chapter 2 we have looked at a number of different ways in which language use varies from person to person and from community to community. A key theme has been that this variation is linked to identity – that the way we use language relates to the way the community in which we live or from which we come uses language. And because of this, the simple act of speaking (irrespective of what we actually say) will indicate something about our social and regional background, as well as our relationship to the person we're speaking to.

An important point to add though is that language variation is *dynamic*. As communities alter (as people move from place to place, as culture changes under the influence of the media or because of particular social or historical events), the language used by the community will also alter. Furthermore, people aren't locked in to using a particular dialect simply because that was the predominant speaking style of the place they grew up. People can and do tailor their language to the situations in which they find themselves. As we saw with Amy Tan, people often shift between different language styles for different audiences. In the next Language Studies chapter (Chapter 6) we'll further explore some of these ideas by looking at the way that language relates to the context in which it is used, and at how people exploit linguistic conventions for the purposes of expression. Before that, however, we'll look at how the structures of spoken language and conversation can be drawn on in creative writing in the construction of dialogue and the creation of the narrator's voice.

# 5 Inventing dialogue

## Narrators and characters

In this section, you are going to look at a short story in which the narrator is one of three characters. This means you will be looking at two different aspects of the story – how the narrator speaks when she is narrating, and how the characters (including the narrator) speak to each other. You need to be alert to the way in which the writer, Mary Robison, has developed the voices, and to think about how she hopes or expects the reader to react. Plainly, a story involves much more than voice – it involves structure, time, theme, plot (the ordering of the events in the story). The characterisation will come from what the narrator and characters do as well as what they say. But for the moment, let's concentrate on their voices.

---

### ACTIVITY

Read 'Pretty Ice' by Mary Robison, which follows. It will be best to read the story twice – in the first instance, simply read through it as you would with any story. After this go back, and see what details you notice about how the narrator and the characters speak, and what these details reveal.

---

### READING: 'Pretty Ice' by Mary Robison

I was up the whole night before my fiancé was due to arrive from the East – drinking coffee, restless and pacing, my ears ringing. When the television signed off, I sat down with a packet of the month's bills and figured amounts on a lined tally sheet in my checkbook. Under the spray of a high-intensity lamp, my left hand moved rapidly over the touch tablets of my calculator.

Will, my fiancé, was coming from Boston on the six-fifty train – the dawn train, the only train that still stopped in the small Ohio city where I lived. At six-fifteen I was still at my accounts; I was getting some pleasure from transcribing the squarish green figures that appeared in the window of my calculator. 'Schwab Dental Clinic,' I printed in a raveled backhand. 'Thirty-eight and 50/100.'

A car horn interrupted me. I looked over my desktop and out the living-room window of my rented house. The saplings in my little yard were encased in ice. There had been snow all week, and then an ice storm. In the glimmering driveway in front of my garage, my mother was peering out of her car. I got up and turned off my lamp and capped my ivory Mont Blanc pen. I found a coat in the semidark in the hall, and wound a knitted muffler at my throat. Crossing the living room, I looked away from the big pine mirror; I didn't want to see how my face and hair looked after a night of accounting.

My yard was a frozen pond, and I was careful on the walkway. My mother hit her horn again. Frozen slush came through the toe of one of my chukka boots, and I stopped on the path and frowned at her. I could see her breath rolling away in clouds from the cranked-down window of her Mazda. I have never owned a car nor learned to drive, but I had a low opinion of my mother's compact. My father and I used to enjoy big cars, with tops that came down. We were both tall and we wanted what he called 'stretch room.' My father had been dead for fourteen years, but I resented my mother's buying a car in which he would not have fitted.

'Now what's wrong? Are you coming?' my mother said.

'Nothing's wrong except that my shoes are opening around the soles,' I said. 'I just paid a lot of money for them.'

I got in on the passenger side. The car smelled of wet wool and Mother's hair spray. Someone had done her hair with a minty-white rinse, and the hair was held in place by a zebra-striped headband.

'I think you're getting a flat,' I said. 'That retread you bought for the left front is going.'

She backed the car out of the drive, using the rear-view mirror. 'I finally got a boy I can trust, at the Exxon station,' she said. 'He said that tire will last until hot weather.'

Out on the street, she accelerated too quickly and the rear of the car swung left. The tires whined for an instant on the old snow and then caught. We were knocked back in our seats a little, and an empty Kleenex box slipped off the dash and onto the floor carpet.

'This is going to be something,' my mother said. 'Will sure picked an awful day to come.'

My mother had never met him. My courtship with Will had happened in Boston. I was getting my doctorate there, in musicology. Will was involved with his research at Boston U., and with teaching botany to undergraduates. 'You're sure he'll be at the station?' my mother said. 'Can the trains go in this weather? I don't see how they do.'

'I talked to him on the phone yesterday. He's coming.'

'How did he sound?' my mother said.

To my annoyance, she begun to hum to herself.

I said, 'He's had rotten news about his work. Terrible, in fact.'

'Explain his work to me again,' she said.

'He's a plant taxonomist.'

'Yes?' my mother said. 'What does that mean?'

'It means he doesn't have a lot of money,' I said. 'He studies grasses. He said on the phone he's been turned down for a research grant that would have meant a great deal to us. Apparently the work he's been doing for the past seven or so years is irrelevant or outmoded. I guess "superficial" is what he told me.'

'I won't mention it to him, then,' my mother said.

We came to the expressway. Mother steered the car through some small windblown snow dunes and down the entrance ramp. She followed two yellow salt trucks with winking blue beacons that were moving side by side down the center and right-hand lanes.

'I think losing the grant means we should postpone the wedding,' I said. 'I want Will to have his bearings before I step into his life for good.'

'Don't wait too much longer, though,' my mother said.

After a couple of miles, she swung off the expressway. We went past some tall high-tension towers with connecting cables that looked like staff lines on a sheet of music. We were in the decaying neighborhood near the tracks. 'Now I know this is right,' Mother said. 'There's our old sign.'

The sign was a tall billboard, black and white, that advertised my father's dance studio. The studio had been closed for years and the building it had been in was gone. The sign showed a man in a tuxedo waltzing with a woman in an evening gown. I was always sure it was a waltz. The dancers were nearly two stories high, and the weather had bleached them into phantoms. The lettering – the name of the studio, my father's name – had disappeared.

'They've changed everything,' my mother said, peering about. 'Can this be the station?'

We went up a little drive that wound past a cindery lot full of flatbed trucks and that ended up at the smudgy brownstone depot.

'Is that your Will?' Mother said.

Will was on the station platform, leaning against a baggage truck. He had a duffle bag between his shoes and a plastic cup of coffee in his mittened hand. He seemed to have put on weight, girlishly, through the hips, and his face looked thicker to me, from temple to temple. His gold-rimmed spectacles looked too small.

My mother stopped in an empty cab lane, and I got out and called to Will. It wasn't far from the platform to the car, and Will's pack wasn't a large one, but he seemed to be winded when he got to me. I let him kiss me, and then he stepped back and blew a cold breath and drank from the coffee cup, with his eyes on my face.

Mother was pretending to be busy with something in her handbag, not paying attention to me and Will.

'I look awful,' I said.

'No, no, but I probably do,' Will said. 'No sleep, and I'm fat. So this is your town?'

He tossed the coffee cup at an oil drum and glanced around at the cold train yards and low buildings. A brass foundry was throwing a yellowish column of smoke over a line of Canadian Pacific boxcars.

I said, 'The problem is you're looking at the wrong side of the tracks.'

A wind whipped Will's lank hair across his face. 'Does your mom smoke?' he said. 'I ran out in the middle of the night on the train, and the club car was closed. Eight hours across Pennsylvania without a cigarette.'

The car horn sounded as my mother climbed from behind the wheel. 'That was an accident,' she said, because I was frowning at her. 'Hello. Are you Will?' She came around the car and stood on tiptoes and kissed him. 'You picked a miserable day to come and visit us.'

She was using her young-girl voice, and I was embarrassed for her. 'He needs a cigarette,' I said.

Will got into the back of the car and I sat beside my mother again. After we started up, Mother said, 'Why doesn't Will stay at my place, in your old room, Belle? I'm all alone there, with plenty of space to kick around in.'

'We'll be able to get him a good motel,' I said quickly, before Will could answer. 'Let's try that Ramada, over near the new elementary school.' It was odd, after he had come all the way from Cambridge, but I didn't want him in my old room, in the house where I had been a child. 'I'd put you at my place,' I said, 'but there's mountains of tax stuff all over.'

'You've been busy,' he said.

'Yes,' I said. I sat sidewise, looking at each of them in turn. Will had some blackish spots around his mouth – ballpoint ink, maybe. I wished he had freshened up and put on a better shirt before leaving the train.

'It's up to you two, then,' my mother said.

I could tell she was disappointed in Will. I don't know what she expected. I was thirty-one when I met him. I had probably dated fewer men in my life than she had gone out with in a single year at her sorority. She had always been successful with men.

'William was my late husband's name,' my mother said. 'Did Belle ever tell you?'

'No,' Will said. He was smoking one of Mother's cigarettes.

'I always like the name,' she said. 'Did you know we ran a dance studio?'

I groaned.

'Oh, let me brag if I want to,' my mother said. 'He was such a handsome man.'

It was true. They were both handsome – mannequins, a pair of dolls who had spent half their lives in evening clothes. But my father had looked old in the end, in a business in which you had to stay young. He had trouble with his eyes, which were bruised-looking and watery, and he had to wear glasses with thick lenses.

I said, 'It was in the dance studio that my father ended his life, you know. In the ballroom.'

'You told me,' Will said, at the same instant my mother said, 'Don't talk about it.'

My father killed himself with a service revolver. We never found out where he had bought it, or when. He was found in his warm-up clothes – a pullover sweater and pleated pants. He was wearing his tap shoes, and he had a short towel folded around his neck. He had aimed the gun barrel down his mouth, so the bullet would not shatter the wall of mirrors behind him. I was twenty then – old enough to find out how he did it.

My mother had made a wrong turn and we were on Buttles Avenue. 'Go there,' I said, pointing down a street beside Garfield Park. We passed a group of paper boys who were riding bikes with saddlebags. They were going slow, because of the ice.

'Are you very discouraged, Will?' my mother said. 'Belle tells me you are having a run of bad luck.'

'You could say so,' Will said. 'A little rough water.'

'I'm sorry,' Mother said. 'What seems to be the trouble?'

Will said, 'Well, this will be oversimplifying, but essentially what I do is take a weed and evaluate its structure and growth and habitat, and so forth.'

'What's wrong with that?' my mother said.

'Nothing. But it isn't enough.'

'I get it,' my mother said uncertainly.

I had taken a mirror and a comb from my handbag and I was trying for a clean center-part in my hair. I was thinking about finishing my bill paying.

Will said, 'What do you want to do after I check in, Belle? What about breakfast?'

'I've got to go home for a while and clean up that tax jazz, or I'll never rest,' I said. 'I'll just show up at your motel later. If we ever find it.'

'That'll be fine,' Will said.

Mother said, 'I'd offer to serve you two dinner tonight, but I think you'll want to leave me out of it. I know how your father and I felt after he went away sometimes. Which way do I turn here?'

We had stopped at an intersection near the iron gates of the park. Behind the gates there was a frozen pond, where a single early morning skater was skating backward, expertly crossing his blades.

I couldn't drive a car but, like my father, I have always enjoyed maps and atlases. During automobile trips, I liked comparing distances on maps. I liked the words latitude, cartography, meridian. It was extremely annoying to me that Mother had gotten us turned around and lost in our own city, and I was angry with Will all of a sudden, for wasting seven years on something superficial.

'What about up that way?' Will said to my mother, pointing to the left. 'There's some traffic up by that light, at least.'

I leaned forward in my seat and started combing my hair all over again.

'There's no hurry,' my mother said.

'How do you mean?' I asked her.

'To get William to the motel,' she said. 'I know everybody complains, but I think an ice storm is a beautiful thing. Let's enjoy it.'

She waved her cigarette at the windshield. The sun had burnt through and was gleaming in the branches of all the maples and buckeye trees in the park. 'It's twinkling like a stage set,' Mother said.

'It is pretty,' I said.

Will said, 'It'll make a bad-looking spring. A lot of shrubs damaged and turn brown, and the trees don't blossom right.'

For once I agreed with my mother. Everything was quiet and holding still. Everything was in place, the way it was supposed to be. I put my comb away and smiled back at Will – because I knew it was for the last time.

(Robison, 1992 [1977], pp. 434–9)

## DISCUSSION

I wonder if you spotted how appropriate the title, 'Pretty Ice', is to Robison's narrator, Belle. From the outset, Belle is frosty. There is something tetchy about how she depicts the intrusion her fiancé's arrival represents (she is more interested in her accounting). She dislikes her mother's 'compact' car, complains about her own new shoes, is grumpy about the tire (tyre) on her mother's car, about her mother's humming, the 'girlish' extra weight put on by Will, the way her mother accidentally honks the horn, the ink-spots on Will's mouth, her mother's suggestion that Will stay in Belle's old room, the way her mother gets lost. In fact, the writer has used Belle's voice to depict her as hostile and negative. (What is skilful about the story is that we are given the option of attributing this to lack of sleep, before discovering that the likely cause is her father's suicide fourteen years earlier, and allowing us to hazard that he, like Belle, has been something of a depressive.) Notice how much of the strength of this story comes from Robison's manipulation of Belle's voice as a narrator. When a creative writer is developing a voice, the voice needs to be consistent in tone, in what we might call attitude.

In the next section, we will return to Robison's story, looking in particular at dialogue, and how this can be developed.

# Dialogue

**Dialogue**, in creative writing, is the term we give to what takes place when two or more characters are speaking. It is fairly rare to find several characters talking in the same scene, even when there are many characters in a novel, play or film. It is rarer still on radio (because it is difficult for listeners to follow) and also rare in short stories, which tend to focus on a few characters and a relatively short space of time (as 'Pretty Ice' does). This isn't to say that it never happens – for instance, the key scene in Ken Loach's film *Land and Freedom* (1995), written by Jim Allen, occurs when about twelve characters noisily debate – in three or four languages – whether the land in a village during the Spanish Civil War should be made public property. There is a similar, lively debate, in Timberlake Wertenbaker's play *Our Country's Good* (1988), when, in one scene, several army officers discuss the merit of theatre in a penal colony in Australia. But writing dialogue for so many characters is generally to be avoided, as it makes excessive demands on the audience. In both *Land and Freedom* and *Our Country's Good*, the scenes in which many people are talking are conspicuous by being unusual. If you want to make dialogue work, you need to restrict it to two, three, or sometimes four characters.

As noted in Chapter 3, dialogue never copies real-life conversation. It simply takes on the air of real-life conversation. The novelist and screenwriter Sol Stein makes this point (Stein is often aggressively assertive, as this extract suggests):

> If you need proof that dialogue and spoken words are not the same, go to a supermarket. Eavesdrop. Much of what you'll hear in the aisles sounds like idiot talk. People won't buy your novel to hear idiot talk. They get that free from relatives, friends, and at the supermarket.
>
> (Stein, 2003 [1995], p. 113)

As Stein also observes, good dialogue in a story (for any medium) needs to be 'oblique' – that is, to contain indirect responses. You might think that Stein is overstating the case, and I would agree that it is easy to derail writing by never creating a straightforward conversation. But I think he's crucially right about the opening sallies in fictional dialogue. This does not mean that every line has to stray in a surprising direction, but it does mean that platitudes need to be avoided – perhaps especially at the outset of a scene. In 'Pretty Ice', there are exchanges that would look like this if laid out as a script for a play or film:

BELLE:    I think you're getting a flat. That retread you bought for the left front is going.

MOTHER:    I finally got a boy I can trust, at the Exxon station. He says that tire will last until hot weather.

and

MOTHER:    Why doesn't Will stay at my place, in your old room, Belle? I'm all alone there, with plenty of space to kick around in.

BELLE:    We'll be able to get him a good motel.

In the first exchange, notice how Mother does not exactly answer Belle, and in the second exchange, how Belle diverts her away from the question entirely. The dialogue in 'Pretty Ice' moves away from 'real' conversation in the way it is edited and presented to us by the writer. The exchanges are not there to replicate small talk but to invite us to speculate about character. Nor does Robison, in either case, use any verb other than 'said' (although she does say that Belle says the line about the motel 'quickly, before Will could answer'. Arguably, Robison does not need to add this qualification. The words themselves imply it.)

In getting us to speculate about character, of course, Robison is advancing the story, since it is a fundamental of most good storytelling that character drives it. And one of the principal ways of defining a character in a text is by his or her voice.

---

## ACTIVITY

Imagine an exchange between two characters in which the first character's opening line is: 'How are you doing?' See if you can come up with a riposte to this relatively harmless-looking opening remark – a riposte implying that there is more going on in the exchange, and that there is more to find out.

## DISCUSSION

An answer like 'Very well, thank you' will stop any piece of writing dead in its tracks. A more intriguing answer would be indirect, evasive, or (superficially) not apparently an answer at all, as we saw in the discussion of adjacency pairs in the previous chapter. Think about the following suggestions, and compare them with your own.

### Exchange (a)

FIRST CHARACTER:      How are you doing?

SECOND CHARACTER:     You haven't heard what they say.

### Exchange (b)

FIRST CHARACTER:      How are you doing?

SECOND CHARACTER:     I see you have a new friend.

### Exchange (c)

FIRST CHARACTER:      How are you doing?

SECOND CHARACTER:     It looks as if one of us is in trouble.

In each exchange, the innocuous opening conversational gambit is derailed by the reply. This is not to imply that creative dialogue consists of characters refusing to answer questions, or being deliberately obtuse. A conversation that consisted entirely of stand-offs would become tedious. All the same, dialogue has to do more than establish the act of speech. The interaction of the voices has to move a story on, and make the reader or audience want to move on with it. You may want to try repeating the activity with different opening lines, for example: 'Would you like a lift home?' or 'This is the first time I've been here'.

There are other features of the dialogue in 'Pretty Ice' that are worth noticing. As you looked through the story for the second time, you may have noticed that there are clear differences between the ways in which the characters speak. The most conspicuous is that the mother asks questions, or at any rate speaks interrogatively. There are seventeen question marks in her part of the dialogue (by comparison, Will asks three, and Belle only one). This does not mean that Robison has drawn up a table to add up the incidence of questions: but it does mean she can hear her characters speaking, that she has a sense of how they manage conversation. Excluding the moment when Belle and Will are briefly alone together, the mother makes twenty-six interventions, Belle only thirteen. We can infer from this that the mother is a much more talkative and inquisitive person, while Belle is more reserved and even frosty. The mother is also more likely to initiate a line of conversation – as when, despite her promise not to mention Will's problem with his grant, she starts a conversation about just that. I think it is fair to infer that the mother is a naturally chatty individual, and also a little nervous about silence, as some people are. And we can go further with the statistical analysis. Although this is a very inexact science, and if we exclude the exchange at the station between Will and Belle again (when the mother is pretending not to listen, in Belle's opinion), the mother speaks forty-eight sentences to Belle's twenty-nine, and only seven of the mother's forty-eight sentences exceed twelve words, while six of Belle's twenty-nine do. On balance the mother, who speaks 291 words, uses shorter sentences than Belle, who speaks 225 words. At one point, Belle is – in the dialogue – noticeably silent, which the mother never is. Were this a stage or radio play, or a film, we would notice these discrepancies even more.

What makes the story work, in other words, is that there is a contrast between the ways in which the characters speak, and that this, as much as our understanding of Belle through her narration, is what reveals character. Stories tend to work through dialogue: voices are what move a story on, what give us important clues about the participants.

## ACTIVITY

Bearing in mind what we have just discussed, invent a dialogue between two people, perhaps discussing a third person. Make the dialogue about 300 words long, and try to make sure that there is a contrast in the way the characters speak. Think about varying the way in which they construct their sentences, the kinds of phrases they might use, the frequency with which they talk. You don't have to distinguish them by age or gender, but you may find it helpful to do so. It doesn't matter whether you lay it out as in a script, or as in a piece of prose.

## DISCUSSION

It is quite likely that you have created a conversation which has some tension (that is to say, you have made it dramatic). You may also have found that you have written an out-and-out argument. It is worth saying that, in creative writing, perhaps unlike life, it is hard to sustain a fully blown argument for very long. Shouting-matches are hard to sustain, and they are actually not very easy for an audience to hold on to. In 'Pretty Ice', the argument is there beneath the surface. The effect of introducing a third person (as with Will in 'Pretty Ice') into a verbal feud of any sort is to make the argument more complex. This is because – and this is easier to recognise in a stage, radio or screen drama than it is in fiction – it is likely that one of the three will be silent. Silence, however, is a great weapon for creative writers to use. If someone is present but saying nothing, they may actually be contributing to the tension. Indeed, if there are only two people, and one of them is silent (and this does happen in arguments!), the silence is just as important as what is said. If you know the Shakespeare plays *Othello* and *King Lear*, there are very good examples of this. At the conclusion of the final scene of *Othello*, the villain, Iago, is silent for over sixty lines; in the long opening scene of *King Lear*, the villain Edmund, apart from some polite, rather embarrassed remarks at the opening, is silent throughout all the events that take place. The task for the actor who interprets these lines, and for an audience too, is: why is this character so silent? And this question leads us neatly to the concept of subtext.

# Subtext

In the activities above, you were creating not only text but **subtext**. Subtext is what the conversation beneath the words is communicating (both between characters, and to the reader/audience). The subtext of Belle's remark to her mother about the supposedly faulty tyre in 'Pretty Ice', for instance, is that Belle considers her mother to be generally incompetent. It might also be said to mean 'You irritate me, as ever'.

Harold Pinter identified subtext very clearly, in a much-cited speech in 1962 to the National Student Drama Festival, at a time when his plays were repeatedly described as being about 'a failure of communication'.

> There are two silences. One when no word is spoken. The other when perhaps a torrent of language is being employed. This speech is speaking of a language locked beneath it ... The speech we hear is an indication of that which we don't hear. ... I think that we communicate only too well, in our silence, in what is unsaid, and that what takes place is a continual evasion, desperate rearguard attempts to keep ourselves to ourselves.
>
> (Pinter, 1991, p. xiii)

Notice that Pinter refers to two kinds of subtext – the implication of characters not speaking, and there being silence; and the implication of what they actually mean when they are speaking. While Pinter might be regarded as having made the art of meaningful silence his own, he is making an important point. What a character says does not necessarily coincide with what he or she means. Or as Pinter put it, 'under what is being said, another thing is being said' (Pinter, 1991, p. xii).

A clear example of subtext occurs in Woody Allen's film comedy *Annie Hall* (1977), when the two characters Alvy (played by Woody Allen) and Annie (played by Diane Keaton) first meet. The exchange between them is accompanied on-screen by subtitles (shown in the transcript below in italics), which reveal what they are really thinking. The context for the conversation is a discussion about photography.

ALVY:    They're ... they're ... they're wonderful, you know. They have ... they have, uh ... a ... a quality.

*(You are a great-looking girl)*

ANNIE:    Well, I-I-I would ... I would like to take a serious photography course soon.

*(He probably thinks I'm a yo-yo)*

ALVY:    Photography's interesting, 'cause, you know, it's – it's a new art form, and a, uh, a set of aesthetic criteria have not emerged yet.

*(I wonder what she looks like naked?)*

ANNIE:    Aesthetic criteria? You mean, whether it's, uh, a good photo or not?

*(I'm not smart enough for him. Hang in there)*

(Allen and Brickman, 2000 [1982], pp. 39–40)

What we have here is both an acknowledgement and a parody of subtext – which can be much more complex than Allen's examples. Allen is having fun with the idea that chat-up lines conceal doubts and desires. But subtexts can rarely be reduced to such simple phrases. Often there is a complicated and even contradictory pattern of meaning below the surface for an actor, an audience or a reader to interpret.

When writing creatively, in any genre, it is important to have some sense of the sub-text in your head. What is your character really saying? Perhaps it is important here to say that you do not need to have an absolutely precise interpretation in your head, or a parallel set of statements that constitutes the subtext. As the screenwriter Jules Feiffer remarks:

> Working with subtext is not a matter of working it out with notes on it. It's a matter of understanding perfectly what's really going on, what's not going on and why it's not, and how much of it will show on the surface ... You have to leave some [of the subtext] for the audience to work out for itself ... as a member of an audience [I] love to be forced to think and be challenged.
>
> (Seger, 1990, p. 171)

In the same interview, Feiffer remarks that he has 'often been surprised by what my characters have had to say to each other. You get them going and they take off on their own.' Many writers discover their characters in the process of creating them. And writers of scripts for stage, screen or radio give their scripts to actors and directors for interpretation, just as writers of fiction, non-fiction and poetry surrender their voices to readers.

---

## ACTIVITY

Read the following extract from Caryl Churchill's short play *Three More Sleepless Nights* (1980). In it, a couple, Margaret and Pete, are discussing Margaret's previous relationship, with her husband Frank. What do you think they are really saying to each other? What possible subtexts does the exchange between them contain?

MARGARET:   I was so insecure, that was part of it.

PETE:   You had no life of your own.

MARGARET:   I was just his wife. I wasn't a person.

PETE:   You can't blame him though, I mean.

MARGARET:   I don't. I don't any more. I'm sorry for him.

PETE:   Yes, I'm sorry for him.

MARGARET:   He's still drinking. He hasn't changed.

PETE:   You're the one who's changed.

MARGARET:   I've changed. I was just his wife before. I had no life.

(Churchill, 1990, p. 266)

## DISCUSSION

There are many ways of reading this extract, as actors would have to do. As perhaps you have noticed, the dialogue here is interesting because it is a little unpredictable – as when Pete says 'You can't blame him', after apparently having begun by echoing Margaret's words. You may well have questioned the extent of Pete's sincerity. And you may have noticed that the text shows us that the voices are distinctive: Margaret is more animated, Pete rather laconic. In part this is because Pete only gives us single sentences. The pattern of their language is different.

The contrast between the characters is what Churchill, as a writer, has provided. As a playwright, even though she has in her career frequently worked closely with directors and actors at the formative stage of her plays, Churchill is working in a genre that obviously involves handing over her material for interpretation. She cannot be present at every performance, advising 'I meant it to be said like this.' She has to allow not only the actors but an audience their freedom to interpret the work – and this includes interpreting the meaning of the subtext in the dialogue.

---

Less obvious, but just as important, is that creative writers in other genres – in prose, in poetry – also have to reach a stage in which they hand over their texts for interpretation by readers. You can indicate a subtext as a writer, and it is important that you do, but you cannot reach the stage where a reading of your text is definitive. Readers always bring their own experiences and prejudices and personalities to a text.

One strategy for retaining control of the meaning might be for prose writers to add more direction, for instance by the use of verbs and adverbs. We could take the first line above, and transpose it into prose as follows:

> 'I was so insecure, that was part of it,' murmured Margaret wistfully, the tears beginning to well up in her eyes.

The trouble is that, once you, via your narrator, interpret the voices for the reader, your text will start to become unwieldy. It will be so filled with signals that you will crowd your reader out. The sentence I've just created is a poor one, because it not only tells you that it is murmured, but also that it is wistful, and that it is practically lachrymose (and, incidentally, notice how 'in her eyes' is redundant – tears have nowhere else to well up). Having a sense of your subtext is important, but repeatedly defining it for the reader is to be avoided – a prose writer, like a dramatist, has to relinquish ownership.

## ACTIVITY

Create a short dialogue between two people (two contributions from each) in which what they say is not precisely what they mean. It doesn't matter whether you do this in the style of fiction or as a piece of drama. When you have finished, write down what you think was going on beneath the conversation – in the subtext. You might choose to do this the other way round, incidentally – write the subtext first, and then turn it into dialogue.

## DISCUSSION

One thing you will notice immediately is that this is harder to do in prose than it is in stage or film drama. In drama, fewer words will usually be required, because the actors – whether instructed to do so by a stage direction, or by a director, or through their own interpretation – will be able to hint at subtext by using body language, and by altering the tone and timbre of their voices. In film, because of the use of close-ups, it is possible to have significant 'conversations' with very few words being spoken.

As an actor and as a director, the American star Clint Eastwood has made a career out of 'speaking silences', as has the French actress Isabelle Huppert. Sometimes quite banal dialogue (as it may seem on the page) can be highly charged in film. Film is, by its nature, a highly visual medium, and there are many films in which there is little or no dialogue for protracted stretches of time. Because the image offered by the film clarifies the setting and context for the dialogue, it obviates the need for a great deal of the dialogue itself.

In prose fiction on the other hand, you have to supply the context, and give the reader some insight into what the character may be thinking. As noted above, you don't have to use adverbs and powerful verbs to do this. You can use a narrative technique which allows you to look into a character's head, and to hear their thoughts – in effect, a kind of subtext being brought to the surface for the reader's inspection. Here is an invented example:

> 'Do you want to come with me to the station?'
> 'Of course.'
> They climbed into the car. It was not, Sarah knew, the wisest decision. Her father would use the journey to start one of his interminable debates about why women, and Sarah's mother in particular, were addicted to shopping. But why shouldn't her mother go shopping? She heard her father clearing his throat for a predictable monologue. She would let it all wash over her.

We are seeing here what Sarah really thinks: 'But why shouldn't her mother go shopping?' We don't even need the phrase 'she thought'. We will look again at this narrative technique, which is called **free indirect speech**, in Chapter 7.

# Voices from real life

Life writers – autobiographers and biographers – have an interesting challenge in that, when they are creating the voices of people who actually lived, they have to achieve a degree of fidelity to the original. Since none of us possesses perfect recall, these voices are going to have to be re-created. In effect, life writers have much the same task as writers of prose fiction: they have to edit any re-created dialogue so that the speech is believable and gives an insight into character. A great deal of life writing sits interestingly on the fence between fiction and fact, and life writing is often distinguishable from fiction only by its stated intention. There are many novels that have been discovered later to have been highly autobiographical, and many autobiographies that have subsequently turned out to have played fast and loose with the truth. But prose life writing borrows the skills of structure, characterisation, narrative and voice from fiction. And as you have seen from the discussion of the Nixon-Haldeman tapes in Chapter 3, a great deal of editing may be needed to make it comprehensible as well as interesting.

In this final section of the chapter, we will look at examples of life writing that have elected to remain faithful to what has been recorded and transcribed. 'Oral history' – the recording of voices by social historians, most notably Charles Parker – has a sixty- or seventy-year history: that is, over a period when equipment became portable, and from a time when the BBC radio services first became interested in presenting the dialects of different regions. Creative writers have found this process interesting and fruitful for a variety of reasons, just as the opening up of the Mass-Observation archives from the 1980s onwards has also led to numerous life writing anthologies and works of fiction.

---

### Charles Parker

Charles Parker was a radio producer with the BBC who was a key figure in the creation of oral histories. He recorded the words of working men and women for radio programmes, most notably *Radio Ballads* between 1958 and 1963, in collaboration with the folk musicians Ewan MacColl and Peggy Seeger.

### Mass-Observation

Mass-Observation (which still exists, although without its hyphen) was an organisation founded in 1937 by Tom Harrisson, Charles Madge and Humphrey Jennings to record the opinions of volunteer diarists on a range of social issues. Its archive is at the University of Sussex. It is of interest to creative writers as well as social historians: perhaps the most well-known product of its archive was *Housewife, 49* (2007), Victoria Wood's television adaptation of the diaries of Nella Last. In 2008, the Mass-Observation archive became available online.

---

One of the attractions of recorded speech is the authority of authenticity. Many writers – especially film-makers – invest their works with authority by stating (or at any rate alleging) that the events to be witnessed are based on 'a true story'. Films such as *De-Lovely* (2004), a biopic of the composer Cole Porter, or *Pierrepoint* (2005), a portrait of Britain's most famous executioner, carry with them the cachet of 'truth'. It is not hard to show that both of these, like most films declaring themselves to be 'based on the truth', contain conflations, changes of focus or date and inventions or distortions of actual fact. But that they carry extra authority because they claim to speak to us with a degree of truth is part of their appeal.

In contrast to the above examples, **oral history theatre** and **verbatim theatre** are extremely conscientious about fidelity. 'Oral history theatre' is an overarching term used to describe drama that uses transcripts to a greater or lesser degree. 'Verbatim theatre' is a more specific term used of drama that is almost entirely constructed from transcripts and, occasionally, public documents.

The writer Rib Davis has used material spoken by real people to create scripts for stage, radio and television. The next activity, which uses some of Rib Davis's work, will give you the opportunity to look at how a transcript of a person's original words might be transformed into a piece of drama.

## ACTIVITY

Read the transcript below, which describes a car crash.

JILL: We were going like the clappers in this beaten-up old thing, I don't think it had ever done this speed in its life before, and Cherry had got her head out the window yelling at all the passers-by and Sheila and Penny were in the back shouting things like 'Is this all it can do?' 'Put your foot down' – but my foot was flat on the floor as it was, I mean we were determined to get to the cinema before the thing started and, well it was fun too, I mean it felt really great … all of us together … And then – well you know this – the tyre blew, the front tyre on the driver's side, and there wasn't time to say anything, not even … well I mean maybe someone said, 'Oh God' or something but I don't remember any screaming, though there may have been, I think we just sort of clung on – to whatever – just sort of clung on, and first we went all over the road and then we went off into this ditch and you could feel the balance going and we went over, and over, and over, and then we stopped … And then there was a moment, well I say a moment, I don't know how long it was – but thinking, 'I'm still alive. I'm still here.' And then we all started checking that we were all there. And we were, God knows how, especially Cherry, who'd had her head out the window. She was in hospital for three months, traction, on her back, but she was alive. The front window, the windscreen, it came out in one piece – I suppose it's meant to do that, and we all crawled out of that. We didn't deserve to be alive, I suppose.

(Davis, 2008, pp. 186–7)

Imagine that you have to present this story as a dramatisation of between two and four minutes' duration in a stage play. What might you do to make it interesting for an audience? You can make some notes or, if you would prefer, produce a short piece of script.

Now read the text that Davis has created by transforming the transcript into a piece of drama. What tactics has he used?

*JILL, CHERRY, PENNY and SHEILA face the audience.*

JILL:     The front window, the windscreen, it came out in one piece – I suppose it's meant to do that, and we all crawled out of that.

*JILL, CHERRY, PENNY and SHEILA take up positions as though in a car. JILL is driving, CHERRY has her head out of the window and SHEILA and PENNY are in the back. They are all obviously enjoying themselves.*

SHEILA:     *(yell – as though over the sound of the engine)* We –

PENNY:     *(yell)* – were –

SHEILA:     *(yell)* – going –

JILL:     Like the clappers!

PENNY:     – in this beaten-up old thing.

JILL:     I don't think it had ever done this speed in its life before, and Cherry –

CHERRY:     Yoohoo!!

JILL:     – had got her head out of the window.

PENNY:     *(to JILL)* Is this all it can do?

SHEILA:     *(to JILL)* Put your foot down!

JILL:     It's flat on the floor as it is!

CHERRY:     We're going to get there before it starts!

SHEILA:     And it was fun.

JILL:      It felt great!

PENNY:    All of us together!

*All freeze. This is held for a few moments, and then while the others stay frozen, JILL turns to us.*

JILL:      I don't remember any screaming, though there may have been.
           Someone may have said 'Oh God.'
           A tyre'd blown.
           We just sort of clung on.

*PENNY and SHEILA slowly turn to us, but CHERRY remains frozen.*

PENNY:    Sort of clung on ...

SHEILA:   Clung onto ...

JILL:      Clung onto whatever.

*Now suddenly all, including CHERRY, are totally unfrozen, and screaming, as together they turn over and over. All lie still, silent.*

JILL:      And I thought, 'I'm still alive. I'm still here.'

*(slight pause)*

           You there?

PENNY:    Yeah.

SHEILA:   Yeah.

*(slight pause)*

JILL:      Cherry?

*(slight pause)*

JILL:      Cherry was still there, God knows how.

CHERRY:   I was in hospital for three months, traction, on my back. But I was alive.

(Davis, 2008, pp. 188–9)

## DISCUSSION

There are about 300 words in the transcript, of which about half find their way into the finished scene. Many of the other words are implied by or even reproduced in the stage directions, e.g. 'together they turn over and over'. Very occasionally a grammatical tense is changed: otherwise, what we have here are the original words.

However, Davis has turned the original monologue into dialogue, shared between four characters, who sometimes echo each other ('clung on … clung on …'), and who sometimes address each other, and sometimes address the audience. This device gives the script far greater energy than the original transcript, an energy which you will note in the dramatisation. Not only that, the order in which the words taken from the transcript are used is quite different. And they also come to us in brief sections (the longest speech is only twenty-five words). What Davis has done is to dramatise the transcript by editing it, by changing its context and by multiplying the voices. Repetitions and pauses have also been added to give the piece greater tension and drama, as have the actions, such as the mime of rolling over. The example here shows us that, while transcripts are often unwieldy, it is possible to use sections of 'real' language – by presenting it, edited, and by adapting it to fit the artifice of theatre. As Davis comments, 'In real life four women would never divide a sentence up between them like this ['We – were – going – like the clappers'], but this is theatrical dialogue, not real life' (2008, p. 189). You may have been tempted to present the original transcript as a single voice, perhaps edited. But a stage adaptation requires greater speed, more activity, more for the audience to focus upon.

What is interesting about Davis's work is that it operates with integrity: wherever possible, he involves those whose writing he has transcribed in the process of staging a play. Verbatim theatre takes further this desire to be faithful to the source material. Philip Ralph's play *Deep Cut* (2008), for example, which concerns the alleged suicide of a young army private at Deepcut Barracks, takes great pains to use almost no word that cannot be found in the transcript of an interview, a newspaper, radio or television report, parliamentary records or in the text of an inquiry. Nevertheless, Ralph has a play to write. He may not alter the words, but he edits them together, conflates occasional characters and stitches the many excerpts together into a coherent whole. This should alert you to the fact that writing is very much a process of adaptation as well as imagination, as much about structure and editorial work as about inspiration.

---

In this chapter, we have looked at some of the ways of creating dialogue, and of transforming 'real life' into something more arresting, something that contributes to the power of story. At every step, you will notice that writing is about more than invention: more properly, it is about adaptation and transformation. At the heart of each act of creation is the process of editing. In the next two chapters, you will be reading first about the way in which linguists look at the concept of genre (which has a slightly different meaning to the one discussed earlier), and of how language is closely related to the context in which it is used. We will then move into a closer study of the contexts in which creative writing takes place and how you can shape language to give a sense of time and location.

# 6 Writing and register

## Language as a tool

In the first two Language Studies chapters we looked at the ways in which language is determined by its users, and at how the phenomenon of dialect plays an important role in people's identities. We examined how differences in language use occur from social group to social group (i.e. different groups have different dialects), and we observed that all language use is to some extent systematic and follows set patterns of use. In the Creative Writing chapters we've looked further at how distinctive voices – the idiosyncrasies in the patterns in which people speak – can be used to create characters. In this chapter we move on to the subject of language that is determined by the uses to which it is put rather than by the geographical or social background of the people who use it. This type of language is called a register, and is another fundamental aspect of everyday communication. **Register** is another way in which *how* something is said or written can be as important for the meaning of the message as *what* is said or written.

Let's begin by considering the metaphor of language being a tool. Like a tool, language is used for getting things done. We use language to ask for things, to explain things, to give instructions, to apologise, to make people laugh, and so on.

---

### ACTIVITY

Take a few minutes to make a list of what you have used language to do so far today. How many different tasks have you achieved by means of language? Would you have been able to achieve these without recourse to speaking or writing?

### DISCUSSION

So far today I've done a variety of things using language. These range from greeting members of my family, to answering emails, to reading a book on the train on the way home. I've held meetings with colleagues, both in person and by phone; and at lunchtime I used language to order a sandwich. Plus, of course, I've been sitting in front of the computer writing this chapter. In fact, I'd say that the majority of my day so far has involved using language. I've used both spoken and written forms of language, some instances of which have taken a lot of effort to produce (e.g. the drafting of this chapter), and some of which I've done practically without thinking (the greetings, the ordering of lunch). In each case, I've had a particular objective I've been trying to fulfil. And without having recourse to language – and to the various forms of communication technology which act as a medium for my use of language (pen and paper, telephone, computer, etc.) – I'd have been able to achieve virtually none of these things.

---

The metaphor of language being a tool was notably used by the philosopher Ludwig Wittgenstein in the middle of the twentieth century. In describing language in this way, Wittgenstein shifted the study of language away from the abstract analysis of its structure to the way it is actually used – and especially to the question of what it is used for. Prior to this, most mainstream linguistics had concentrated on describing the various components of a language and how these parts fit together. Linguists spent the majority of their time cataloguing and analysing the grammatical workings of different languages, and generalising rules about this structure. Wittgenstein's writings – particularly his book *Philosophical Investigations* (1953) – were instrumental in shifting the focus of attention to what language is used to achieve.

In proposing this view of language, he writes: 'Think of the tools in a tool-box: there is a hammer, pliers, a saw, a screw-driver, a rule, a glue-pot, glue, nails and screws. – The functions of words are as diverse as the functions of these objects' (Wittgenstein, 1953, para. 11). A corollary to this view of language is that, if we want to get something done, we need to use the *correct* tool. For example, we can't successfully bang a nail into a wall with a screwdriver. Or at least we could, but it wouldn't be the most efficient way to achieve the objective, and could easily end with us damaging ourselves or ruining the job. The same applies to the use of language. We need to use the right type of language for the right type of activity. And what counts as the right type of tool will depend on the task at hand and the circumstances in which it is to be used.

Take, for example, the task of writing an essay. If you are writing an essay as a part of a course you are studying, you need to ensure that you use the correct tone of language, that you employ the right vocabulary (including the use of any specialised terminology), and that you follow the appropriate structuring and formatting conventions (i.e. that you include an introduction and conclusion, you have a central argument, you reference any works you may quote, etc.). All these are elements of an **academic register**, and they are part of the toolkit you use to express yourself in an academic environment. It would be inappropriate, for example, to write an academic essay using the same type of language that you use for writing a text-message to a friend. Not only would it give the wrong impression to the teacher or tutor, but the type of language would not allow you to discuss the complex concepts and issues that are involved in academic study. In effect, using the wrong type of language would not get the job done properly.

In this chapter we'll look at what comprises a register, and at how people use different registers in their everyday lives. In doing this, we'll concentrate, for the most part, on examples of written language. We'll examine how different activities determine the type of language used for that activity, and at how written texts frame our expectations about their meaning from the way they conventionally organise information. Language defined by its use is also a feature of spoken discourse of course, and the chapter will also discuss a few examples of spoken interaction drawn both from real-life settings and from literature and drama. In fact we'll begin by looking at the differences between spoken and written language. As you will see, the distinction between spoken and written language is also in part a result of the different purposes to which these two ways of using language are put. In other words, speech and writing are different tools that we use for different types of task.

## Differences between speech and writing

If you were asked what the difference is between speech and writing you might well reply that the answer is startlingly obvious: one involves making a variety of sounds with your voice, while the other involves making marks on a piece of paper or on a screen. They both use identical forms of language, you may say; the difference between them is just a matter of the means by which that language is actually transmitted. To an extent such an answer is perfectly correct. In modern British society – and in many other societies – a large proportion of the population mostly use the same language, i.e. English, when speaking and writing. But as we saw in the previous chapter, within the broad category of 'English' there can be great variety in the way people actually use the language, and this variety is systematic (i.e. it has a regularity to it, and is not random or arbitrary) and related to the social environments in which people live. One question we could ask, therefore, is whether similar variety exists between the spoken and the written **modes** of language use. (The word 'mode' refers to the means by which a message is communicated. Different modes include speaking, writing, or – in the case of sign language – gesture.) Are speaking and writing identical in all aspects except for the fact that one uses the voice and the other the alphabet? Or is there something fundamentally different not only in the mode of expression but also in the form of the language they require?

The answer to this partly lies in the nature of the mode used to transmit the message. As I mentioned above, whenever we use language we do so in combination with another sort of tool, such as a computer, a phone, a pen or simply our own voice. If I want to write a letter, I need pen and paper, plus a system that will ensure that my letter is delivered to the person to whom it is addressed. And it is usually the case that the type of language we use in any given situation will be influenced by the type of tool we use. This influence can be seen not only in the obvious superficial differences between speaking and writing (the former involves modulations of sound in the atmosphere; the latter involves marks on a page or screen), but also in the way that the communicative message is structured.

When writing a letter, for example, I have to take into account the fact that the person to whom I am writing is not physically present and so cannot respond or ask for clarification about what I'm trying to convey. I also have to take into account that the recipient will not read the letter for a day or two, so I need to be explicit about things like time and place. All these points will affect the way I compose the message, with the result that, even if the general content of the message is much the same as it would have been if I'd been able to talk directly to the person, the actual shape of the message will be very different. In other words, speech and writing are likely to have different structures because they are used for different communicative purposes, and because they allow for different communicative possibilities.

---

## ACTIVITY

Look at the two short pieces of discourse below. Which of them do you think was originally spoken, and which was written? What features of the language led you to decide which category to put them in?

### Example 1
Connected speech is like a set of boxes within boxes. The focuses of consciousness (lines), most of which are single clauses, are grouped together as one large, unitary body of information, like the setting of a story. This larger body of information is itself composed of stanzas, each of which takes a single perspective on an event, state of affairs, or character.

(Gee, 2005, p. 128)

### Example 2
last yesterday
when my father
in the morning

an' he …
there was a hook
on the top of the stairway
an' my father was pickin me up
an' I got stuck on the hook
up there
an' I hadn't had breakfast
he wouldn't take me down
until I finished all my breakfast
cause I didn't like oatmeal either
(Gee, 2005, pp. 127–8)


## DISCUSSION

Example 1 is a piece of written discourse (although the topic is about speech!). It is from an academic book – one about Language Studies, as it happens. Example 2 is a transcript of a piece of spoken discourse. It is an extract from a short narrative by a seven-year-old girl from the USA. There are a number of differences between the two extracts. The first concerns the way that they are laid out on the page. Example 1 is set out in a way that is conventional for written texts. Each sentence follows directly after the previous one, and they are separated by full stops. Each new sentence begins with a capital letter, and the different phrases within it are marked off by commas. Example 2, on the other hand, doesn't follow these conventions. There is no use of formal punctuation rules; instead phrases (or rather, short chunks of meaning) are distinguished by a line break.

There is also a difference in the type of vocabulary used, and in how the words are strung together. Example 1 is more complex in this respect. It uses standard spelling, along with phrases such as 'unitary body of information', and it nests clauses inside one another to allow for a level of precision in the meaning it is expressing, e.g. 'The focuses of con-sciousness (lines), most of which are single clauses, are grouped together'. Example 2 uses a far less intricate structure of clauses. The structure basically involves one small chunk of the story following directly on from another. We can almost see the path of the meaning unfolding before us, as the speaker wends forward with the narrative, occasionally making wrong turns and needing to correct herself. The result is a burst of short, repetitive phrases, some of which are ungrammatical, and some of which simply get abandoned halfway through.

Part of the reason why Example 2 is less complicated is because the speaker is a young child. But it is also because spoken language relies much more on the capabilities of our memory, whereas written language allows for a more considered approach to the composition. In writing we can take time picking out the right word, and ensuring that all the grammatical elements of the sentence agree with one another and that the meaning flows in a smooth and coherent way. In other words, in written discourse we can edit our utterances in a way which simply isn't possible in spoken discourse. (And this ability to *edit* is, as we have seen, crucial to the process of *creative* writing.)

---

### Transcripts

As we noted at the beginning of the book, all the 'spoken' language in the book has been written down. In other words, Example 2 in the previous activity is a **transcript** of actual speech. It is still a representation of speech, in much the same way that the extracts from the novels and plays in Chapter 2 were (the extracts by Mark Twain, J.M. Synge, and George Bernard Shaw). But whereas the extracts from literature in that chapter were invented approximations of how people speak (i.e. they were fabricated examples of language use – of the sort discussed in the Creative Writing chapters), this transcript is a record of a real instance of speech. We can mark this distinction by saying that the literary examples – especially the extracts from the plays – are **scripts**, whereas this real-life example is a transcript. The intention of a transcript in the context of Language Studies is to document as accurately as possible what was said, in such a way that the person reading it can get a clear impression of what was going on. For this reason, things like pauses, overlaps or misspoken words are often included. The transcripts from the Watergate tapes, and that used by Rib Davis in the previous chapter, also record actual speech, but because they are not intended to be used for linguistic analysis, they do not document every pause, false start and overlap in such detail. And as we saw in Chapter 3, when creative writers represent 'authentic' speech, they often ignore or stylise these types of features, and create something (a script) that gives the impression of being naturalistic, but in fact is not.

## Register: language defined by its use

Comparing examples of spoken and written discourse shows us that the structure of language can be influenced by the way it is used. The basic difference between spoken and written language is simply that one uses the voice and the other the pen or computer. It is no more complicated than that. But the implications of these different modes – that communication using the voice is likely to be more immediate, more reliant on the context in which it occurs and on the human capabilities of the speakers, and that communication using pen or computer often allows for more deliberation and is more permanent – result in a range of marked differences in the structure of the language.

In what other ways, then, does language differ according to the uses to which it is put? The simple answer is: in a great variety of ways. Much as there is huge diversity in the dialects of English, so also there is great diversity in the different registers of the language. And just as the diversity and variety of dialects complicates simplistic ideas about what English is, so the same thing applies to the concept of different registers. For example, it may be that, although you consider yourself to be a highly proficient English speaker, there will be certain situations where you will struggle to understand what people are talking about simply because you are not used to the register of language they are using. The Russian literary critic Mikhail Bakhtin writes that:

> Many people who have an excellent command of a language often feel quite helpless in certain spheres of communication precisely because they do not have a practical command of the generic forms used in the given spheres. Frequently a person who has an excellent command of speech in some areas of cultural communication, who is able to read a scholarly paper or engage in a scholarly discussion, who speaks very well on social questions, is silent or very awkward in social conversation.
>
> (Bakhtin, 1986, p. 78)

Bakhtin is here suggesting that different types of communicative encounter (different 'generic forms' of communication) have different rules and conventions, and that one needs to know these in order to operate successfully in particular situations. You may have experienced something similar yourself. Whereas you might be perfectly competent in certain areas of social life when it comes to communicating in English, in other areas you might find yourself suddenly less confident and feel that your language is 'letting you down'. For example, you may feel entirely comfortable talking in great detail about a sport or hobby, but when speaking to a mortgage adviser you may find yourself struggling to understand vital terms or feeling self-conscious about the style of language you are using. Or perhaps in your case it is the opposite, and you can talk happily about financial issues but struggle if the conversation turns to football.

---

## ACTIVITY

Look at the following two extracts, both of which are from written commentaries of sports matches. Both these texts were published by major news networks and both are in contemporary English. To what extent can you understand them? Are there any words you don't understand – either because they appear completely new to you, or because they seem to be used in an unfamiliar way?

## Extract 1

The Dodgers made it 3–1 in the bottom of the third when Ethier was hit by a pitch, moved up on a walk to Ramirez and took third on James Loney's flyout.

Third baseman Mark DeRosa made a diving, backhanded stop of Blake's infield hit down the line, but his throw to second sailed into right field. In the second, DeRosa banged his right hand into Loney while scrambling back to first base on a lineout.

Wolf let St. Louis load the bases with no outs in the first. But he allowed just one run on Ryan Ludwick's bloop single to center between Kemp and Ronnie Belliard, and then Kemp put Los Angeles ahead.

(Harris, 2009)

## Extract 2

1158: Aus 356–6. Fred will have one more, at least. That's nightmarish to face – pinging up from short of a length and crashing in to Johnson's bat handle – but that's well played, pulled off his nose for two to deep midwicket. 166 needed by Australia, and Johnson is settling in a little – 26 not out, hogging the strike from his more experienced pardner.

1204: Aus 356–7. Drift and dip did for Clarkie there – Swann gave it some air, Pup got monkeyed in the flight and the ball then turned just enough from outside off to thunk the top of the off peg. As bowling changes go, that's useful …

1229: He's starting to look a little weary now, Fred – Siddle jabs down on two in-dippers and gets the second down to long leg for a single. Johnson defends one away, takes a single off the fifth and exposes Siddle to what could be Flintoff's last ball. In-swinging yorker dug out – no-ball, so he'll have another pop. He turns off a run-up of about 10 paces – BOWLED HIM!

(Fordyce, 2009)

## DISCUSSION

Extract 1 is a report from the Associated Press on a baseball game from the USA; Extract 2 is part of an online commentary from the BBC about a cricket match: the second Test in the Ashes series at Lord's in 2009. If you're familiar with these sports and their rules, you'll probably have understood the passages easily enough. If you don't know much about the sports, they probably didn't make much sense to you.

Extract 1 is full of specialist terminology. The first sentence, for example, includes the fol-lowing terms: 'The Dodgers made it 3–1 in *the bottom of the third* when Ethier was *hit by a pitch, moved up on a walk* to Ramirez and *took third* on James Loney's *flyout.*' In addition, you'd need to know whom the proper names refer to (the Dodgers, Ethier, James Loney), and what the significance of a 3–1 score is. If all the information that requires this specialist understanding were to be removed, we would be left with practically nothing that is meaningful. So although the passage is in English, and it uses fairly simple words such as 'third' and 'walk', the way it uses these words constitutes a specialist register, and can seem baffling if you aren't familiar with that register.

Extract 2 is similar. Again, there is a lot of specialist terminology, such as 'short of a length', 'long-leg' and 'in-swinging yorker'. In addition, the writer assumes a great deal of shared knowledge with his readership. For example, players are referred to by nicknames (Fred, Clarkie), and the style of the language is very colloquial and full of slang terms that refer to specific elements of the game (e.g. 'Pup got monkeyed in the flight'). There is also a sense in this passage that the writer is playing with language – for example in using a spelling such as 'pardner' instead of 'partner' – which also conveys a sense of familiarity with the readership. So again, to understand this passage you need a knowledge of the technical vocabulary of cricket, a knowledge of the way players are referred to among this community of fans, and a knowledge of the type of slang that is being used. If you are familiar with the context in either case, the texts will be easy to follow. But if you aren't, they could well appear almost nonsensical, despite the fact that they are both written in English.

---

Both the above examples are instances of specialised uses of language associated with particular activities. As such, both texts are addressed to particular groups of people: baseball fans and cricket fans respectively. We could say, therefore, that they are addressed to two particular *communities* of people, each of which share an interest in the respective sports and, in pursuing this interest, have come to share a particular way of talking about these sports. In other words, they are both communities that use a particular register of language as a result of their shared interest in a particular activity. In Language Studies, such a group is known as a **discourse community**.

The linguist John Swales lists the following elements as being central to the idea of a discourse community (1990, pp. 24-7):

1. the existence of a shared set of goals

2. the use of an established mechanism of communication between members

3. the use of a specialist vocabulary, and of particular genres of communication

4. the existence of a core set of members who have an expertise in this use of language.

Communities of this sort may not interact face to face, or be located in a single geographical area. But their shared interest in a particular subject or activity means that their distinctive use of language still constitutes an important aspect of their behaviour, and as such is part of their identity.

## ACTIVITY

The reading below is an example that Swales gives of a discourse community to which he himself belongs. Read the passage, and as you do so, think about the role language plays in the way the members of the community relate to each other. Does this community adhere to the other conditions that Swales has identified as being defining elements of a discourse community?

## READING: An example of a discourse community

The discourse community is a hobby group and has an 'umbrella organization' called the Hong Kong Study Circle, of which I happen to be a member. The aims of the HKSC (note the abbreviation) are to foster interest in and knowledge of the stamps of Hong Kong (the various printings, etc.) and of their uses (postal rates, cancellations, etc.). Currently there are about 320 members scattered across the world, but with major concentrations in Great Britain, the USA and Hong Kong itself and minor ones in Holland and Japan. Based on the membership list, my guess is that about a third of the members are non-native speakers of English and about a fifth women. The membership varies in other ways: a few are rich and have acquired world-class collections of classic rarities, but many are not and pursue their hobby interest with material that costs very little to acquire. Some are full-time specialist dealers, auctioneers and catalogue publishers, but most are collectors. From what little I know, the collectors vary greatly in occupation. One standard reference-work was co-authored by a stamp dealer and a Dean at Yale; another was written by a retired Lieutenant-Colonel. The greatest authority on the nineteenth century carriage of Hong Kong mail, with three books to his credit, has recently retired from a lifetime of service as a signalman with British Rail. I mention these brief facts to show that the members of the discourse community have, superficially at least, nothing in common except their shared hobby interest ...

The main mechanism, or 'forum' (Herrington, 1985) for intercommunication is a bi-monthly Journal and Newsletter, the latest to arrive being No. 265. There are scheduled meetings, including an Annual General Meeting, that takes place in London, but rarely more than a dozen members attend. There is a certain amount of correspondence and some phoning, but without the Journal/Newsletter I doubt the discourse community would survive. The combined periodical often has a highly interactive content as the following extracts show:

2. Hong Kong; Type 12, with Index
No one has yet produced another example of this c.d.s. that I mentioned on J.256/7 as having been found with an index letter 'C' with its opening facing downwards, but Mr. Scamp reports that he has seen one illustrated in an auction catalogue having a normal 'C' and dated MY 9/59 (Type 12 is the 20 mm single-circle broken in upper half by HONG KONG). It must be in someone's collection!

3. The B.P.O.'s in Kobe and Nagasaki
Mr. Pullan disputes the statement at the top of J.257/3 that 'If the postal clerk had not violated regulations by affixing the MR 17/79 (HIOGO) datestamp on the front, we might have no example of this c.d.s. at all.' He states that 'By 1879 it was normal practice for the sorter's datestamp to be struck on the front, the change from the back of the cover occurring generally in 1877, though there are isolated earlier examples'; thus there was no violation of regulations.

My own early attempts to be a full member of the community were not marked by success. Early on I published an article in the journal which used a fairly complex frequency analysis of occurrence – derived from Applied Linguistics – in order to offer an alternative explanation of a puzzle well known to members of the HKSC. The only comments that this effort to establish credibility elicited were 'too clever by half' and 'Mr Swales, we won't change our minds without a chemical analysis'. I have also had to learn over time the particular terms of approval and disapproval for a philatelic item (cf. Becher, 1981) such as 'significant', 'useful', 'normal', and not to comment directly on the monetary value of such items.

Apart from the conventions governing articles, queries and replies in the Journal/Newsletter, the discourse community has developed a genre-specific set of conventions for describing items of Hong Kong postal history. These occur in members' collections, whether for display or not, and are found in somewhat more abbreviated forms in specialized auction catalogues, as in the following example:

> 1176   1899 Combination PPC to Europe franked CIP 4 C canc large
> CANTON dollar chop, pair HK 2 C carmine added & Hong Kong
> index B cds. Arr cds. (1) (Photo) HK$1500.
>
> Even if luck and skill were to combine to interpret PPC as 'picture postcard', CIP as
> 'Chinese Imperial Post', a 'combination' as a postal item legitimately combining
> the stamps of two or more nations and so on, an outsider would still not be in a
> position to estimate whether 1500 Hong Kong dollars would be an appropriate
> sum to bid. However, the distinction between insider and outsider is not absolute
> but consists of gradations. A professional stamp dealer not dealing in Hong Kong
> material would have a useful general schema, while a member of a very similar
> discourse community, say the China Postal History Society, may do as well as a
> member of the HKSC because of overlapping goals.
> The discourse community I have discussed meets all ... the proposed defining
> criteria: there are common goals, participatory mechanisms, information
> exchange, community specific genres, a highly specialized terminology and a high
> general level of expertise.
>
> (Swales, 1990, pp. 27–9)

## DISCUSSION

Swales states that this group meets all the criteria for a discourse community as he has outlined them. As we can see from the examples from the newsletter, the community uses a specialised register, full of technical terminology ('PPC' and 'CIP'), which is mostly incomprehensible to the outsider. (It's worth noting that discourse communities don't necessarily need to have *such* specialised interests.) The group is geographically dispersed across the globe, and the members rarely if ever meet face to face, but instead communicate by means of the journal and newsletter. There is a core of expert members, and new members wishing to participate need to adapt their own linguistic practices to the community's norms (which was something Swales himself had to do, and found rather challenging at first). And of course, they have a common goal, which acts as the *raison d'être* for the community.

As we can see then, one of the key functions of a specialist register is to allow people to communicate with a high level of precision. Specialist terms, such as those used by stamp collectors, allow for the discussion of phenomena that non-specialists would not be concerned with. But as was also touched upon above, registers are not only used for the transmission of factual information. They can also express what is known as 'interpersonal meaning'. That is, they can be a means of communicating something about the identity of the speaker or writer. For example, the use by a doctor of a specialist register can be a way of indicating his or her professional identity. The ability to use a phrase such as 'tibial shaft fracture' rather than 'broken leg' points to membership of the medical community. In this way, register is a type of identity marker in much the same way that dialect is. But whereas dialect is related to geographical or social background, register is related to occupation or specialism, and to the part of people's identity that concerns what they do rather than where they are from.

The next activity contains examples of text that has appeared in the guidance notes, or 'small print', of various commercial services. They have been collected together by the Plain English Campaign, a society that, in its own words, campaigns 'against gobbledygook, jargon and misleading public information' (Plain English Campaign, 2010). They are all examples of what the Plain English Campaign considers to be unnecessarily complicated uses of English.

---

## ACTIVITY

Read Examples 1–3, then try to 'translate' them into 'plain' English. Is anything lost in the translation? Why might these statements have been written in the way that they are?

### Example 1

If there are any points on which you require explanation or further particulars we shall be glad to furnish such additional details as may be required by telephone.

### Example 2

It is important that you shall read the notes, advice and information detailed opposite then complete the form overleaf (all sections) prior to its immediate return to the Council by way of the envelope provided.

### Example 3

This Agreement and the benefits and advantages herein contained are personal to the Member and shall not be sold, assigned or transferred by the Member.

## DISCUSSION

The Plain English Campaign supplies the following 'translations' for these three extracts:

### Example 1
If you have any questions, please phone.

### Example 2
Please read the notes opposite before you fill in the form. Then send it back to us as soon as possible in the envelope provided.

### Example 3
Membership is not transferable.

Their versions are certainly much clearer than the originals, and manage to avoid any unnecessary words or phrases. But is anything lost by simplifying these statements like this? It probably depends on what we think the purpose of the statements is. One element of their purpose is to communicate basic factual information. But they are probably also intended to convey a certain impression to their readership. And the use of this rather complex (and perhaps pompous) register helps to do this. In other words, using phrases such as 'we shall be glad to furnish such additional details as may be required' is probably intended to lend a certain gravitas to the expression.

# Genres of communication

So far we have looked at how choices about vocabulary and grammatical structure are used in the production of meaning. Another important aspect of meaning is the way a piece of discourse is organised at a more general level. To describe this aspect of the organisation of a text, we use the term **genre**. As was mentioned earlier, this is a term which has slightly different meanings in different contexts. For example, in the disciplines of Literature, Creative Writing and Music it refers to different categories or types of work, such as, in the case of Literature and Creative Writing: tragedy, sonnet or short story; and, in the case of Music: symphony, concerto or opera. The same general meaning applies in Language Studies, but here the term refers to *any* type of communicative act. It can refer to both a written text and to forms of spoken inter-action. So, for example, in Language Studies a letter is referred to as a particular type of genre, as is an academic essay, an everyday conversation or a political speech. In each case, there are conventional patterns in the way the communicative act is organised. And because of these conventions, we already have a general framework in which to interpret the meaning of a communicative act simply by recognising the genre it is in.

Take, for example, the way you read a letter. Before you get to the first sentence you already know, based simply on the way it looks, that it is a letter – and indeed, you probably know what sort of letter it is. Because you know this, you can probably make rough inferences about what the content is going to be. If it is on headed paper, for example, and laid out with an address printed in the top corner, it is more likely to be a business letter than a personal note from a friend. As we can see then, the genre creates certain expectations about the communication, and is a means of framing the content inside.

---

## ACTIVITY

The reading below is an extract from an essay by Mikhail Bakhtin. We looked at a short passage from this reading earlier. Here you have a chance to read it again within the context of his argument that all communicative language use is framed in genres. While reading, think about how his argument ties in with our discussion above about how a letter is a type of communicative genre. Can you think of further common genres of communication?

---

## READING: The problem of speech genres

We speak only in definite speech genres, that is, all our utterances have definite and relatively stable typical *forms of construction of the whole.* Our repertoire of oral (and written) speech genres is rich. We use them confidently and skillfully *in practice*, and it is quite possible for us not even to suspect their existence *in theory*. Like Molière's Monsieur Jourdain who, when speaking in prose, had no idea that was what he was doing, we speak in diverse genres without suspecting that they exist. Even in the most free, the most unconstrained conversation, we cast our speech in definite generic forms, sometimes rigid and trite ones, sometimes more flexible, plastic, and creative ones (everyday communication also has creative genres at its disposal). We are given these speech genres in almost the same way that we are given our native language, which we master fluently long before we begin to study grammar. We know our native language – its lexical composition and grammatical structure – not from dictionaries and grammars but from concrete utterances that we hear and that we ourselves reproduce in live speech communication with people around us. We assimilate forms of language only in forms of utterances and in conjunction with these forms. The forms of language and the typical forms of utterances, that is, speech genres, enter our experience and our consciousness together, and in close connection with one another. To learn to speak means to learn to construct utterances (because we speak in utterances and not in individual sentences, and, of course, not in individual words). Speech genres organize our speech in almost the same way as grammatical (syntactical) forms do. We learn to cast our speech in generic forms and, when hearing others' speech, we guess its genre from the very first words; we predict a certain length (that is, the approximate length of the speech whole) and a certain compositional structure; we foresee the end; that is, from the very beginning we have a sense of the speech whole, which is only later differentiated during the speech process. If speech genres did not exist and we had not mastered them, if we had to originate them during the speech process and construct each utterance at will for the first time, speech communication would be almost impossible ...

Many people who have an excellent command of a language often feel quite helpless in certain spheres of communication precisely because they do not have a practical command of the generic forms used in the given spheres. Frequently a person who has an excellent command of speech in some areas of cultural communication, who is able to read a scholarly paper or engage in a scholarly discussion, who speaks very well on social questions, is silent or very awkward in social conversation. Here it is not a matter of an impoverished vocabulary or of style, taken abstractly: this is entirely a matter of the inability to command a repertoire of genres of social conversation, the lack of a sufficient supply of those ideas about the whole of the utterance that help to cast one's speech quickly and naturally in certain compositional and stylistic forms, the inability to grasp a word promptly, to begin and end correctly (composition is very uncomplicated in these genres).

(Bakhtin, 1986, pp. 78–9, 80)

## DISCUSSION

Bakhtin's argument is that *all* our communicative encounters are structured by means of conventional genres of interaction. And yet, he contends, we take these genres completely for granted and so most of the time we don't even notice them. But the way we approach an encounter or communicative act, and the expectations we have about it, are informed by the conventions associated with it.

One good example of a genre of communicative interaction is the job interview. Most job interviews have a standard formula and include a number of specific elements. These range from expectations about how the participants should dress, about how the room is set out and where everyone sits, to how the conversation itself is organised. On a very basic level, the interviewer directs the proceedings, asks questions, takes notes and, at the end, allows the interviewee to ask any questions he or she may have. Throughout the proceedings the language used is polite and mostly formal. All this is taken for granted – it is not explicitly explained when you step into the room for an interview. And if the candidate wants to get the job, he or she has to conform to the genre of the interaction and to know and negotiate these hidden conventions.

In the next activity you will read an extract from an article by Celia Roberts about the structure of job interviews in the UK. It begins with a transcript of part of an interview (which, as you will see, gives quite a detailed blueprint of the dynamics of the conversation), which is followed by Roberts's analysis of how the interaction is structured. The candidate in the example is called Ire. He is from Nigeria, and is being interviewed for a low-paid delivery job. Roberts describes the eventual outcome of his interview as 'Borderline successful'. The analysis she provides is rather complex, so you may need to read the extract more than once. I'll go over the key points she raises in the activity discussion. Roberts suggests that the interview is structured around implicit norms. As you read, think about what the implications of this are for Ire and for the type of responses he gives. The details of this particular communicative genre are more subtle than the very basic formula I outlined above. Roberts writes of the way that British job interviews today are often structured around a 'competency framework' – that is, there are a number of key concepts such as team-working, self-management, good time-keeping, customer focus, etc., that are considered to be important attributes for a good employee. The interviewer will thus ask questions around these concepts, and is looking to see how well the candidate picks up on these.

## ACTIVITY

While reading the extract, consider the following questions. To what extent does Ire manage to pick up on the key concepts that make up a competency framework and present himself as aware of and able to fulfil these criteria? Why might he be at a disadvantage here because of his background?

## READING: Institutional discourse

I:  right what would you tell me is the advantage of a repetitive job (1)       1

C:  advantage of a

I:  repetitive job (1)

C:  er I mean the advantage of a repetitive job is that er:m it makes you it
    it keeps you going, er it doesn't make you bored, you don't feel bored       5
    you keep on going and, I mean I me-a – and also it it puts a smile on
    your face you come in it puts a smile on your face you feel happy to
    come to the job the job will (trust) you

I:  you don't get to know it better

C:  Sorry                                                                       10

I:  you don't get to know it better

C:  yeah we get to know the job better we I mean we learn new ideas lots
    of new ideas as well

I:  right what is the disadvantage of a repetitive job

C:  well, disadvantage er:m, er disadvantages (1) you may you may
    f-offend customers you may f-offend our customers in there that's
    a disadvantage of it                                                        15

I:  you don't find it boring

C:  yeah it could also be boring, to be boring and you- and you, yet
    by being bored you may offend the customers                                 20

I:  how how would you offend them by being bored

C:  by not putting a smile on your face

(Roberts and Campbell 2005: 39)

**Transcript conventions**
I = interviewer
C = candidate
: lengthening of a sound
(1) silence timed in seconds

This short extract exemplifies many of the themes of the selection interview. First, the hidden assumptions of the interviewers serve to construct inequality when there is no shared definition of the interview. Shared inferential processes depend upon 'socially constructed knowledge of what the interview is about' (Gumperz 1992: 303) but there are few explicit clues to this or what candidates' roles and modes of communicating should be. The question in line 1 is designed to elicit a particular competence that relates to self-management. British interviews are now routinely constructed around a competency framework that also includes competencies such as team working, communications, customer focus, adaptability and flexibility. These reflect the discourses of the 'new work order' (Gee *et al.* 1996) in which workers, however low their status in the workplace, are expected to buy into a corporate ideology. Flattened hierarchies require individuals to be autonomous and self-regulating. So the competency questions at lines 1 and 14 are based on a set of conventionalised expectations that repetitive jobs are boring, but that enterprising, self-managing candidates will recognise this and find ways of dealing with the boredom which will maintain their identity as motivated workers. The candidate's requests for clarification, the perturbation phenomena in lines 4 and 5 and the interviewer's rebuttals of his responses in lines 9 and 18 show that he has not cued into the special line of inferencing embedded in this new work order ideology and into the fabric of the interview ...

... Despite Ire's best attempts to interpret the interviewer's questions, he remains a borderline candidate since the misunderstandings displayed create uncomfortable moments that feed into doubts about his acceptability for the job.

The sequential organisation of the interview illustrates its fundamentally asymmetrical character and the role of the interviewer in the final decision-making. Candidates are routinely blamed for what is a joint production (Campbell and Roberts 2007). The interview is controlled almost entirely by the interviewers who govern the interactional norms, allocation of turns and speaking roles (Komter 1991; Birkner 2004). In this extract, the interviewer has a script which she drives through and in which only certain answers are allowable and institutionally processable.

(Roberts, 2010, pp. 193–4)

## DISCUSSION

Roberts writes that the interviewer has certain hidden assumptions about the interview, and that these 'serve to construct inequality when there is no shared definition of the interview'. In other words, although the interviewer has a set understanding of the genre and of what she expects to hear in the answers of a good candidate, the candidate himself is not in possession of this knowledge. The two parties in this interaction don't share the background understanding of what constitutes a successful interview, and because of this, the interviewee is at a distinct disadvantage. So, for example, the opening question is meant to give Ire a chance to talk about how he is able successfully to manage his own work ('self-management' is one of the 'key competencies'). But he is not asked about this in an explicit way, and so doesn't realise that this is what he is meant to be demonstrating in his answer. Part of the reason that he doesn't share the same expectations about the genre as the interviewer is that these are conventions that are current in British interviews, but may not be the same in Ire's home culture of Nigeria. So although the interview is intended to be a fair and neutral assessment of any candidate's potential, instead it ends up being biased towards those who share the same knowledge of genre conventions as the interviewer.

# Comic voices

What happens, then, when expectations about genre or register are broken? In an interview situation, if one mistakes the generic conventions the result will probably be a failure to get the job. In other words, the consequences of not following the (implicit) rules are a breakdown of communication. In some contexts, however, flouting the conventions can be part of the overall act of communication. For example, contravening generic expectations is a device that is often used in the construction of comedy.

Henri Bergson, the French philosopher, who wrote a famous treatise on the nature of comedy (*Laughter: An Essay on the Meaning of the Comic*), suggests that 'A comic effect is always obtainable by transposing the natural expression of an idea into another key' (2004 [1911], p. 61). We can think of the 'natural expression of an idea' as the conventional genre associated with an idea. To transpose it 'into another key' would be to shift from the expected to an unexpected genre or register. Purposely flouting generic expectations, then, can result in what is known as 'register comedy' (Attardo, 1994). This is where one type of register is juxtaposed with another to create something incongruous. Below is a short example from one of the Jeeves and Wooster stories by P.G. Wodehouse. In this extract Bertie Wooster finds himself in a quandary when a friend asks if he could do her a favour. He feels that agreeing to such a request is likely to lead to unwanted intrigue. His valet, Jeeves, is on hand to offer advice:

'If I might make a suggestion, sir?'

'Press on, Jeeves.'

'Would it be possible for you to go to Totleigh Towers, but to decline to carry out Miss Byng's wishes?'

I weighed this. It was, I could see, a thought.

'Issue a *nolle prosequi*, you mean? Tell her to go and boil her head?'

(Wodehouse, 1966, p. 28)

You may not be familiar with the term *nolle prosequi*, unless you have a knowledge of legal terminology. It is a legal concept that comes from the Latin phrase meaning 'refuse to pursue', and is used in common law to describe an application by the prosecution to discontinue criminal charges before the trial. As such, it is part of the register of a specific discourse community – the legal profession – and thus has a sense of formality to it. Bertie, however, undercuts the formal nature of his comment by following up with the phrase 'tell her to go and boil her head'. In terms of straightforward meaning, the two phrases are synonymous – they both mean to refuse to take part in the scheme. But they are poles apart in terms of register, and thus their juxtaposition seems startling, and produces a comic effect.

## ACTIVITY

Let's look at another example of register comedy, a passage from *Hard Times* by Charles Dickens. In the scene below, Mr Gradgrind is giving advice to his daughter, Louisa, about whether she should accept a proposal of marriage from Mr Bounderby. She has asked her father if she should make the decision based on whether or not she loves Mr Bounderby. Mr Gradgrind is a very practical-minded man who is used to engaging in the worlds of business and commerce. The question about love initially throws him, but he regains his composure and responds to his daughter with an analysis of the situation as he sees it. As you read the passage, think about how a clash of registers creates a sense of incongruity. What effect does this have on the serious topic at hand?

'Why, my dear Louisa,' said Mr. Gradgrind, completely recovered by this time, 'I would advise you (since you ask me) to consider this question, as you have been accustomed to consider every other question, simply as one of tangible Fact. The ignorant and the giddy may embarrass such subjects with irrelevant fancies, and other absurdities that have no existence, properly viewed – really no existence – but it is no compliment to you to say, that you know better. Now, what are the

Facts of this case? You are, we will say in round numbers, twenty years of age; Mr. Bounderby is, we will say in round numbers, fifty. There is some disparity in your respective years, but in your means and positions there is none; on the contrary, there is a great suitability. Then the question arises, Is this one disparity sufficient to operate as a bar to such a marriage? In considering this question, it is not unimportant to take into account the statistics of marriage, so far as they have yet been obtained, in England and Wales. I find, on reference to the figures, that a large proportion of these marriages are contracted between parties of very unequal ages, and that the elder of these contracting parties is, in rather more than three-fourths of these instances, the bridegroom. It is remarkable as showing the wide prevalence of this law, that among the natives of the British possessions in India, also in a considerable part of China, and among the Calmucks of Tartary, the best means of computation yet furnished us by travellers, yield similar results. The disparity I have mentioned, therefore, almost ceases to be disparity, and (virtually) all but disappears.'

(Dickens, 1995 [1854], pp. 97–8)

## DISCUSSION

The language and ideas that Mr Gradgrind uses are wholly inappropriate for the nature of the issue, and have the effect of transforming the serious topic into an absurd scene. He engages only in a statistical and economic analysis of the pros and cons of a marriage; what is entirely absent from his speech is the vocabulary of love or romance. And, apart from the opening 'my dear', there is no sign that this is a father speaking to his daughter. So Dickens illustrates the failure of Mr Gradgrind to appreciate the emotional needs of his daughter by giving the character a comically inappropriate response, which is articulated through a highly incongruous register of speech.

It is also worth adding that Dickens himself, as the writer of this passage, is playing with the possibilities of language to produce this effect. We talked at the beginning of the chapter of language being a tool that is used to get things done. Another metaphor we could perhaps use is of language as a toy – that is, something people can play around with, and act on, in a variety of creative ways.

## ACTIVITY

Now let us look at a comic version of a real-life situation you came across earlier: the job interview. Below is an extract from the shooting-script of an episode of *The Smoking Room*, a comedy series originally broadcast on the BBC in 2004. In this scene, three work-colleagues are on their break. One of them, Barry, is about to go for an interview for a promotion. The other two, Lilian and Robin, offer to help him prepare by giving him a practice interview. Read through the script and, as you are doing so, consider how Barry negotiates the expectations of the interview genre.

---

### READING: Extract from shooting script of *The Smoking Room*

LILIAN:   Let's get you ready now.

BARRY:   How?

LILIAN:   Do a dry run! We'll throw some awkward questions out – see how you cope.

*BARRY REACTS*

Well ... some questions.

...

*SHE COMPOSES HERSELF FOR THE MOCK INTERVIEW.*

So! I'm Sharon. [The name of their boss, who will be conducting the real interview.] She won't have a ciggy on the go. Obviously.

*ROBIN AND BARRY NOD, WILLING HER TO HURRY ON.*

Or such good legs!

*SHE'S DISAPPOINTED THAT NONE OF THE MEN BACK HER UP ON THIS.*

ROBIN:   (*TO BARRY*) And you won't have your crossword.

BARRY:   Oh. No.

*IT SHOULD NOW BE APPARENT – IF IT HASN'T BEEN ALREADY – THAT BARRY USES HIS NEWSPAPER AS A SECURITY BLANKET. HE DOESN'T KNOW HOW TO SETTLE WITHOUT IT. HE TRIES FOLDING AND UNFOLDING HIS ARMS, ETC.*

LILIAN:   So, Barry. Thank you for attending this interview.

*THERE'S NO RESPONSE FROM BARRY.*

You should say something back.

BARRY:   Like what?

ROBIN: 'Ta'?

LILIAN: Would it help if he came in through the door?

*BARRY MAKES TO RISE.*

ROBIN: It's not Peer Gynt. Let's skip the first bit – that's just chit chat – he'll be fine with that.

BARRY: Will I?

LILIAN: Why exactly do you want this job?

BARRY: It's a lot more money and I get a desk right by the window.

LILIAN: You can't say that!

CLINT: He's keeping it real.

LILIAN: I think you should keep it unreal. Lie.

*BARRY HAS A LONG THINK THEN CLEARS HIS THROAT.*

BARRY: Well Sharon. It's not like I can't do the job. An orang-utan could do the job. If it was trained in powerpoint and excel. Only, I've always found there are two types of people who get ahead in this life. The first type, sadly, are back-stabbers, net-workers, users. The second I like to think of as … 'shithouses'. And I'm neither. I'm slow, steady Barry. Not the most dynamic of men. Necessarily. So I've had to sit back, watching the most unlikely people get promoted above my head. Promoted to the top in some cases. Well … one case. And it's a joke! Someone needs to stop the rot!

*HE NOW REALISES THAT THIS SPEECH ISN'T GOING DOWN AT ALL WITH THE OTHERS.*

And that's why I'd like this job.

*IT'S A WHILE BEFORE LILIAN OR ROBIN CAN RESPOND.*

LILIAN: Aah. You'll be fine.

ROBIN: Yeah, you'll walk it.

(Dooley, 2004, pp. 33–6)

## DISCUSSION

The answer to the question about how Barry negotiates the expectations of the interview genre is: very badly. He appears unaware of what is expected of his answer, and instead goes off into a completely inappropriate rant about things that annoy him about the job. As this is a comedy, Barry's failure to appreciate the expectations of the genre is much more extreme than in the real-life example we looked at above. And it is the extreme nature of the clash of registers that produces the humour. But central to both the real-life version of the job interview and the comic version is the fact that situations like this have specific rules about how the communication is organised, and that these rules form the frame-work in which the meaning of the encounters themselves then happen. The scene from *The Smoking Room* is comic because Barry's answer is woefully inappropriate; Ire's job application is borderline because he doesn't pick up on the cues to talk about his 'key competencies'.

# Structure and point of view

So far in this chapter we've looked at various ways in which the meaning of an utterance is determined in part by the structure of the language and the way the communication is organised. In this final section we'll look at one further way in which form and structure have an important bearing on the meaning of a text. Our focus here will be on how the choices we make about which words to use and what order to put them in are related to the *perspective* we have towards what we're describing.

A simple example of this is the adage that some people see the glass as 'half full', while others see it as 'half empty'. Both phrases refer to the same physical entity: a glass with a set amount of liquid in it. But the choice of words used to describe this entity indicates two different perspectives on it. The linguist Norman Fairclough refers to this as 'construing reality'. He suggests that the way we describe the world around us contributes to the way we see the world. And the consequence of this is that *no* way of describing the world is entirely neutral. Whenever we describe something, we make particular choices about the vocabulary and grammar we use, and these choices are related to our own specific point of view. In the case of the half full/half empty glass, the perspective is considered to be a sign of one's personality (optimist versus pessi-mist); but in other contexts it could be one's political point of view or one's system of beliefs.

## ACTIVITY

The reading below is from an essay entitled 'Language, reality and power' by Norman Fairclough. In this section of the essay, Fairclough gives an example of how choices over vocabulary play a role in construing the world. The example he picks is, as he notes himself, an extreme case, and it is one that can generate a lot of debate and controversy. What point is Fairclough making in this extract?

## READING: An example of construing

How can we determine when people can be adequately construed as *terrorists*? This is currently sometimes a real problem, for journalists, politicians and ordinary citizens. We need some sense of what counts as *terrorism*, e.g., 'violence with a political and social intention, whether or not intended to put people in general in fear, and raising a question of its moral justification' (Honderich, 2003: 98-9), though not everyone will agree with this definition; and it helps to find clear cases most people could agree on – those who attacked the World Trade Center in New York in 2001 and the London Underground in July 2005 are perhaps pretty uncontentiously *terrorists*.

In some cases we might recognize that people use *terrorist* methods in something like Honderich's sense, and are *terrorists* in some sense, yet feel reluctant because of particular features of the context of their violence to leave it at that and so implicitly equate them with people who are *terrorists* in an unmitigated sense. This might be so with certain acts of extreme violence (e.g., suicide bombings) against Israeli civilians by Palestinians within the *intifada* (though I would unhesitatingly say that, for example, the Palestinians who murdered members of the Israeli team at the Munich Olympics in 1972 were *terrorists*) or by Iraqis in the aftermath of the Iraq War. This is because these actions can be seen as part of a war or insurgency, and are matched by and are responding to acts of comparable violence against civilians by military or paramilitary forces. Note that Honderich's definition is consistent with *state terrorism*, and we might ask why these Palestinians or Iraqis are widely called *terrorists* in the media whereas soldiers using *terrorist* methods are not. I sometimes feel that while such people are *terrorists* in a sense, this is not a fully adequate construal because they are resisting extreme violence, carried out by others who might equally be called *terrorists* but are generally not, so it is also inequitable, but I feel unsure what other word to use, what an adequate construal would be. It's difficult to grasp

> this bit of the world in language – that's the sort of difficulty we quite often have in construing the world, even if this is an extreme example of it.
>
> (Fairclough, 2009, p. 513)

## DISCUSSION

Fairclough maintains that there is no hard-and-fast rule about exactly what type of behaviour constitutes terrorism. For this reason, the word 'terrorist' can be used to describe a range of people acting in different ways, in different contexts and with different motivations. Most people can probably agree on a general definition of the word, but there are instances when different people will interpret actions and events in different ways and thus apply the word to different events. When someone does use the word, however, it immediately classifies the person who is being referred to in a particularly uncompromising and censorious way. So using the word clearly indicates an individual's attitude towards the person and the act he or she has committed, and as such it operates as a political statement about their behaviour.

It is not only choices about vocabulary that create a particular perspective on the way the world is represented. Other choices related to language can also contribute to this. For instance, the syntactical structure of a sentence can be used to foreground certain aspects of the meaning. If, for example, I say: 'The child broke the window with his ball', I am foregrounding the child and his actions. If, on the other hand, I say 'The window was broken by the child's ball', despite the fact that the event described is exactly the same, the actions of the child are now being downplayed. In the second version the window is the subject of the sentence, and thus the child's actions are not stressed as much in the syntax.

Another element that contributes to the perspective of a story is the way other people's words and opinions are reported. This is especially the case in news reports, where the telling of a story often relies on the accounts of participants or witnesses. For example, a report on a football match that includes quotes only from the manager of the losing team might give the impression that the game was marred by bad refereeing and that the final score was a result of a string of bad luck. If the report includes quotes only from the winning manager, on the other hand, the story would probably suggest that the stronger team secured a well-deserved victory.

In the activity below we'll look at an example of how different choices about the language used in the narration of a story give different perspectives on the same event. In early 2010 there was a collision in the Antarctic Ocean between a Japanese whaling ship and an anti-whaling boat belonging to protesters from the environmental group Sea Shepherd. Sea Shepherd said that its boat, the *Ady Gil*, was deliberately rammed by the Japanese ship the *Shonan Maru No. 2*. The crew of the *Shonan Maru*, on the other hand, said that the anti-whaling boat suddenly slowed in front of it and that the collision could not be avoided.

---

## ACTIVITY

Below are the opening paragraphs from two newspaper articles reporting the incident described above. Article 1 is from the Japanese newspaper the *Asahi Shimbun*; Article 2 is from the Australian tabloid *The Daily Telegraph*. Read through the two accounts and consider the ways in which the articles give a different perspective on the incident. Think specifically about the language they use. How do the choices they make about vocabulary, about what aspects of the story they foreground and whose opinions they report, contribute to the overall impression they give of what happened?

### Article 1

#### WHALE SHIP COLLIDES WITH PROTEST VESSEL

An anti-whaling vessel was heavily damaged but its crew were rescued after a collision with a patrol ship for Japanese research whalers in the Antarctic Ocean on Wednesday.

The Fisheries Agency said there was no major damage to the *Shonan Maru No. 2*, which struck the bow of the *Ady Gil*, a 26-ton vessel belonging to the U.S.-based Sea Shepherd Conservation Society, around 12:30 p.m.

Crew members of *Ady Gil* were rescued by another protest vessel sailing in the vicinity.

No crew members aboard the 712-ton *Shonan Maru No. 2* were injured.

' A series of obstructive activities by Sea Shepherd should not be tolerated because they constitute an extremely dangerous act that threatens the lives of the crew,' the agency said.

(*Asahi Shimbun*, 2010)

### Article 2

#### JAPANESE CUT IN HALF ANTI-WHALING SHIP *ADY GIL*

Anti-whaling group Sea Shepherd have confirmed their ship the *Ady Gil* has been rammed and cut in half by Japanese whalers.

According to Captain of the *Steve Irwin*, Paul Watson, the *Ady Gil* – a $1.5 million carbon-fibre stealth boat – was rammed by one of the Japanese security ships.

Mr Watson, who is in charge of one of the three Sea Shepherd vessels trying to interfere with the Japanese whale hunt, told *The Daily Telegraph* the Japanese vessel *Shonan Maru No. 2* rammed the *Ady Gil* and tore off its bow.

'The vessel is taking on water,' he said. 'The captain is still trying to salvage what he can and save his boat. The other five crew members have been rescued.'

The crew were rescued by fellow Sea Shepherd ship the *Bob Barker*.

Capt Watson said the Japanese refused to respond to mayday calls and fled the scene.

The Federal Government is investigating the reports.

(*Daily Telegraph* [Australia], 2010)

## DISCUSSION

If we start by comparing the two headlines we can immediately see a different perspective. Key to this perspective is the choice of verbs: 'Whale ship *collides* with protest vessel' and 'Japanese *cut in half* anti-whaling ship *Ady Gil* [my italics]'. The former suggests something unplanned and maybe accidental; while the latter makes what happened sound much more deliberate. *The Daily Telegraph* article then follows this up by using the word 'rammed' to describe the collision, repeating the word in each of the first three paragraphs. Again, this gives the impression of an intentional and violent action. The *Asahi Shimbun*, on the other hand, repeats its far less evaluative description of a 'collision'.

The two articles also draw on different second-party accounts for the explanation of what happened. The *Asahi Shimbun* includes the opinion of the Japanese Fisheries Agency, while *The Daily Telegraph* quotes the captain of the Sea Shepherd boats. Unsurprisingly there appears to be a bias in both the accounts, which results in very different interpretations of the event. The captain contends that the Japanese refused to answer mayday calls, and that they fled after the incident. The spokesperson for the Japanese Fisheries Agency argues that Sea Shepherd were and continue to be engaged in a series of obstructive activities, which are likely to endanger lives.

The result of the different choices made by the writers about the structure – from small decisions about individual vocabulary items to larger decisions about what to include and what to omit – is that the two articles could almost be about entirely different incidents, such are the discrepancies in the way they appear to see what happened. What is of interest to us, though, is not that different newspapers put different spins on the world, but the role played by language in the way they do this. Texts such as newspaper articles keep us informed about incidents in the world that we don't experience ourselves, and so in this sense we can say that language *mediates* the world around us. And given that much of our knowledge of the world comes from what we hear or read, paying attention to how language is used to represent the world can be an important act of critical awareness.

In this chapter we have looked at language being used for a diverse range of purposes – from telling stories about oatmeal, discussing stamp collecting and reporting on disputes over whaling, to providing commentary on baseball and cricket matches. The common thread throughout has been that the language used in any given context is tailored to the task it is being put to, and that the form and structure of a piece of discourse is an important part of its meaning. In other words, there exist conventions about how language is used in different contexts – and if we want to communicate effectively, we need to become familiar with these conventions and learn how to successfully exploit them.

# 7 Context, time and point of view

## Time, place and genre

In the last chapter, we saw how language use is influenced by the context in which it is used. In creative writing, language is also necessarily influenced by a variety of contexts, and can also be manipulated to create the context itself. Language needs to be manipulated to indicate the time and place in which what you are writing is set. It can also be used to construct the viewpoint which you choose when you are telling a story in much the same way as in the newspaper articles we've just looked at. In a play or (especially) a film, the setting itself can be indicated by scenery or visual effects, although a stage play often relies almost entirely on the language to indicate setting (a radio play may use sound effects). But in all cases, language needs to be adapted to indicate to listener, reader or audience where the action is taking place. Viewpoint, or point of view, shifts according to how you wish to filter the information – externally, or internally, that is from outside the characters, or from within.

Suppose you were to set a short story in Britain in the 1950s. Plainly, it would be very easy to make mistakes, unless you did some research. You can't simply get through by ensuring that you weave into your story details such as Oxydol, Wells' fireworks, the Sobel 21 all-picture TV (86 guineas!), Smedley's tomato ketchup, or Junior Service candy cigarettes. Your story needs a plot, and interesting action and characters. And they need to speak. And in each case, action, character and speech need to be grounded in the everyday routines and patterns of the time.

What would happen if your character wanted to speak to someone on the phone to make a date? In an era where even children have mobile phones, it's hard to imagine (or remember) what it was like. In the 1950s most families didn't have a phone in the home at all (research would show you that it was fewer than 15 per cent at the end of the decade). And this is where your research might lead you astray. Your character would have to make a journey to a public telephone box (bright red), making sure they had a supply of copper coins, lifting the receiver to check there was a tone, and being ready to call a number by inserting a finger in a dial and successively letting it spin back each time from the chosen number. If there was an answer, your character would press 'Button A'. The coins would fall noisily into a metal container. Your character would finally be able to speak, possibly in the knowledge that a queue, members of which could hear much of what was being said, was forming outside. However, it might well be that the public kiosk is not the best way for your character to set up a date. The mistake you would be making here is to concentrate too much on the setting, and not enough on the story.

It is easy to make errors. In the first episode of the British soap opera *Coronation Street* (December 1960), the young lothario Ken Barlow announces to his mother that he is meeting a girl from the other side of Manchester, an arrangement they have made at college. On the morning of the meeting, Ken receives a letter from her confirming their date. I expect you may find that surprising: courtship by letter across the same town has long since vanished. Already, as a creative writer, you will realise that it is very easy to make your setting right, wrong, or downright anachronistic, even when your fiction is set 'only' sixty years in the past. Courtship by letter between teenagers across a short distance would be unthinkable now.

The texture of the language your character speaks is also important. During the broadcast of the TV series *Downton Abbey* (2010– ), which is set in England before, during and after World War I, the scriptwriters were accused of several anachronisms, including the use of the epithet 'get knotted' and the slang phrase 'As if!'. *The Oxford English Dictionary* (*OED*) records the first usage of the former as 1963, and the latter mainly from 1975 (although an American usage is actually logged as early as 1902). Similarly, the author Liz Jensen, when writing *War Crimes for the Home* (2002), was advised that no one in World War II used the phrase 'I should coco', but she decided it was acceptable nonetheless. (And in fact she was right: the *OED* has a variant on it – with 'cocoa' for 'coco' – from 1936, and the *OED* does not record spoken usage, which generally comes first.) These sorts of details all contribute to the overall picture you are creating.

When making decisions such as these, it helps to research the period, of course. There are a number of ways you could do this. You might look at the Mass-Observation material mentioned in Chapter 5, for instance, or at David Kynaston's *Family Britain 1951–1957* (2009). There you would discover examples such as this piece of speech from the period in which a housewife is speaking about her landlord, who is also a church functionary:

> It doesn't encourage you much to go to church, does it, when you see an old skinflint like him! He'd squeeze the last penny out of anybody, and then up he gets on Sundays bold as brass and reads the lessons. I think they're all the same.

Or this of a working-class man speaking about parsons:

> When I had T.B., mate, and was off work for fourteen months I can tell you who looked after me and the missus. It wasn't all these -- -- -- people from the chapel. It was my mates from the boiler shop.
>
> (Kynaston, 2009, p. 532)

By looking at these real-life examples, we learn that an *old skinflint, squeeze the last penny, bold as brass*, and *me and the missus* were in use, and that *mate* and *mates* were current, though perhaps with very slightly different senses. A contemporary writer would be less squeamish, we'd guess, about '-- -- --'. But which expletive was it? Careful! Expletives, as with all slang, are usually very time-specific. There are also other possibilities for research. If you are writing about a period as relatively recent as the 1950s, you might also be able to find an archive online of old radio shows. Or you could interview relatives who were then adults. All that matters is that the language, like the artefacts shown or mentioned, is sufficiently convincing.

However, the further back a writer travels in time, it is the general fluency of the language that needs to be correct. Worrying too much about absolute precision will turn the whole process of creating the speech patterns of your characters into a chaos of cross-referencing. And the more historical the fiction you are creating, the greater the problem with the language. The danger thus becomes producing a cod-version of historical speech patterns, culled from novels and journals of the time. We have no recorded speech from before the 1880s, and precious little until 1900. And in any case, the language used in fiction is often heightened and exaggerated. For example, we don't know if Charles Dickens, composing *Our Mutual Friend* (1865), ever actually heard anyone around him speak like this:

> I am a man as gets my living, and as seeks to get my living, by the sweat of my brow. Not to risk being done out of the sweat of my brow, by any chances, I should wish afore going further to be swore in.
>
> (Dickens, 1971 [1865], p. 194)

What we have here, in the character of Rogue Riderhood, who wants 'an Alfred David' (an affidavit), is a comic, repetitive pastiche of a greedy villain's words. The language is exaggerated, rhythmic, invented, and enjoyable. As with the earlier example from Dickens, it is being used to convey a particular effect.

Let's look at a slightly more tricky example, which we can use to help us think about how we might go about creating a convincing historical context. Here is an extract from Sir Walter Scott's *Rob Roy* (1817):

It was on such a day, and such an occasion, that my timorous acquaintance and I were about to grace the board of the ruddy-faced host of the Black Bear, in the town of Darlington, and bishopric of Durham, when our landlord informed us, with a sort of apologetic tone, that there was a Scotch gentleman to dine with us.

'A gentleman! – what sort of a gentleman?' said my companion somewhat hastily – his mind, I suppose, running on gentlemen of the pad, as they were then termed.

'Why, a Scotch sort of a gentleman, as I said before,' returned mine host; 'they are all gentle, ye mun know, though they ha' narra shirt to back; but this is a decentish hallion – a canny North Briton as e'er cross'd Berwick Bridge – I trow he's a dealer in cattle.'

'Let us have his company, by all means,' answered my companion; and then, turning to me, he gave vent to the tenor of his own reflections. 'I respect the Scotch, sir; I love and honour the nation for their sense of morality. Men talk of their filth and their poverty: but commend me to sterling honesty, though clad in rags, as the poet saith. I have been credibly assured, sir, by men on whom I can depend, that there was never known such a thing in Scotland as a highway robbery.'

'That's because they have nothing to lose,' said mine host, with the chuckle of a self-applauding wit.

(Scott, 1862 [1817], pp. 25-6)

The question we're concerned with here is not the quality of Scott's writing, but whether, in creating historical fiction as a contemporary writer, this is a style to be copied.

## ACTIVITY

If you were writing *Rob Roy* today, as a historical novel (i.e. one set in the early eighteenth century), what aspects of the language in the extract above would you consider changing? You are not being asked to 'update' Scott, but to assume that you are editing it so that it reads as though a contemporary writer had written it.

## DISCUSSION

The language here that presents difficulty for a contemporary reader (were this to be a piece of twenty-first-century historical fiction, and not an actual excerpt from two centuries ago), is I think, far less in the dialogue than in the narrator's words. The characters' speech (i.e. the language used for their own voices) may sometimes seem a little stilted to a modern ear – the phrase 'commend me to sterling honesty, though clad in rags, as the poet saith' is a rather confusing phrase (I don't know from my general knowledge who the poet is, and *saith* is an archaic form of the verb), and 'credibly assured' may seem too formal for our sense of conversation. We also don't use the phrase 'North Briton' or 'hallion' (scoundrel, but probably used here as 'chap') any more, either. Even Scott, rather awkwardly, points out that 'gentlemen of the pad' (highwaymen) was not in current use when he wrote *Rob Roy*.

However, it is the narrator's rather florid phrasing, as in 'he gave vent to the tenor of his own reflections' that causes the greater difficulty. If you were writing a historical fiction set at the time of 'Rob Roy' – Scott is writing about the early 1700s from the viewpoint of the early 1800s – then it would be best to write the narrative itself in contemporary language: perhaps just 'he reflected', in this case. The regional dialect used by the characters in this passage – from the area where Durham and Yorkshire meet in the north of England – might actually work quite well. But an imitation of Scott's style, or an extension of that style into dialogue, would sink the writing immediately. If a historical novel comes close, as it can do, to a pastiche of stereotypically Shakespearean language – full of 'forsooth's and 'prithee's – it will not work. A historical novel needs to be written in contemporary prose, with as little archaism as possible. It is a convention, and arguably true, that conversation was more formal, and generally less expletive-strewn, one or two hundred years ago. But it is all too easy to stilt your language by focusing on some impossible concept of accuracy. It is also a convention that historical fiction is less colloquial than contemporary fiction. And that is fine. This does not mean that fiction from a previous era always avoided the use of colloquialisms and regional accents. It might intrigue you to read the kind of language the character Joseph uses in Emily Brontë's novel *Wuthering Heights* (1849):

> I sudn't shift for Nelly, nasty ill nowt as shoo is. Thank God! shoo cannot stale t' sowl o' nob'dy! Shoo wer niver soa handsome but what a body mud look at her 'bout winking. It's yon flaysome, graceless quean that's witched our lad wi' her bold een and her forrard ways, till – Nay, it fair brusts my heart! He's forgotten all I've done for him, and made on him, and goan and riven up a whole row o' t' grandest currant trees i' t' garden!
>
> (Brontë, 1965 [1849], p. 349)

In summary, then, linguistic detail can help give a feeling for the period you are writing about – and obvious anachronisms will break the illusion. But absolute authenticity of historical speech patterns often isn't necessary, especially in the narration itself, and is likely to weigh the writing down.

# The demands of genre fiction

Whether you're writing steampunk, aga-sagas, chick-lit, sci-fi, vampire fiction, whodunnits, police procedurals, westerns, erotica, or fantasies, the issue is rarely one of language but, as mentioned above, of convention. Often, these conventions are a kind of comfort-blanket for the reader. In other words, the genre produces particular expectations. If I read a novel by crime-writer Ed McBain, for example, I know that it will begin with an establishing series of paragraphs about the weather in New York – too hot, too cold, too wet, and so on – and a corpse. That suits me. I know where I am, and I enjoy it.

You need to have a sense of whom you are writing for, too. And as a writer you must establish a quiet contract with them that you will write in a style of language that does not jar the eye or ear. As noted above, historical fiction makes particular demands. The evidence that you are writing in a different decade, century, or era – and this could be in the future, of course – comes from the detail of the setting, and the items you place in it, far more than the dialogue. How people speak is a matter of making sure that you are not absurdly using language that belongs to an inappropriate time. As an example, *A Place of Execution* (1999), a crime novel by Val McDermid, moves between 1963 (when a murder is investigated) and 1997–1998 (when the murder is solved). In the later time-frame, there are mentions of emails; a Toyota estate car; an Armani suit; and there is a house where there are no ashtrays. The 1963 passages include a dark red Dansette record-player with cream knobs; black-and-white photographs; a 'modern' shag pile carpet that we know instantly is of its time, just from its colours; a Ford Zephyr car; any number of pop-song titles; and smoking is practically constant. These establishing details are not overdone.

In the 1963 dialogue, there are very few instances of words or phrases that are not particularly current, but here are four which you might well hear today, but far more rarely: *cheerio, the bee's knees, a ticking-off, bright as a button*. While we are looking at these four, it's interesting to note that, if you are setting your dialogue in a context you have not lived in, let us say in North America if you yourself are from the UK, the slang is much more difficult to perfect. For example, if you 'tick someone off' in America, you will be annoying them; and 'bright as a button' is far more likely to be 'cute as a button'. As we discussed earlier in the book, patterns of usage such as these differ from community to community. Likewise, if you used 'the bee's knees' in a nineteenth-century context, it would refer to something insignificant, and not 'clever' or 'fashionable' or 'the best': the meaning of the phrase has altered somewhat down through the years. A question you need to ask yourself as a writer is whether anyone would spot an anachronistic use of 'the bee's knees'. I would doubt it.

Val McDermid's novel, when it moves towards the end of the twentieth century, contains dialogue with the following words or expressions that would not have been current in the 1963 section: *hands-on, cyberspace, full of it, run that past me,* and *different scenarios.* I suspect that *panned out* and *on you go* would also not have turned up in colloquial speech in 1963. The point about creating speech styles in dialogue is that you simply need to tread carefully – and also to make sure that you do not make a fetish of filling your dialogue with historical expressions. A little goes a long way.

## ACTIVITY

Here is a short, invented passage of speech. If you were creating dialogue in a modern setting, which words would you feel uncertain or even downright convinced were inappropriate?

> Lumme, she's bangin' at moving – absolutely awesome. Fancy! I want a chin-wag with her asap. I'll ask her to give me a bell, even though I'll probably make a right horlicks of it. Is that the Harry Lime? Oh dash it, I've got to chip.

## DISCUSSION

First, nobody talks like this! Not only are the words from different periods of time, but also from different age-groups and contexts. Some of the phrases have survived a long time; some may be in use, but only in an ironic or parodic way. Language that is considered dead also has a habit of reappearing, sometimes with new meanings. It's a *dead cert* some of this *chuntering* will have *carked it* (died!) within months …

However, in answer to the question: I doubt that *lumme* is in very much use anywhere, and I suspect that *chin-wag* is rare. If anyone still uses *dash it*, it must be ironically, and this may also be true of *Fancy! Moving* in the sense of dancing looks dated to me, too. *Give me a bell*, despite the fact that it relates to obsolete phones, seems to have survived, at least in certain communities; so does a *right horlicks*, and *asap* (sometimes now pronounced *ay-sap*). *Awesome* and *chip* (hurry off) are both current, the first more generally than the second. The same might be said of *bangin'*, although it's a youth-word that may well be on the way out, since youth slang vanishes with great speed. As for *Harry Lime* (Cockney rhyming slang for 'time'), I've never heard it said, but I suspect it's in use. And as with many slang words, it's related to a particular regional community.

This brief exercise will, I hope, convince you that slang is dangerous territory for writers – unless they are using slang with which they are familiar. Trying too hard to keep up with the times will incidentally date your writing.

# The pivotal nature of time in a story

If you look back to the story 'Pretty Ice' in Chapter 5, you will see that it also offers you another very notable aspect of time in story-telling. The action of the story lasts no more than about an hour – from six-fifteen in the morning to about seven-fifteen – before breakfast, at any rate, and however long it takes to drive two miles after about seven o'clock. Yet the story refers to a whole series of moments – moments years earlier when Belle met Will (about seven years ago), and further back to times when the dance studio ('closed for years') was still running, long enough in the past for Belle's mother to note that 'everything has changed'. It incorporates the moment when Belle's father committed suicide, eleven years earlier. It refers to Belle's life in the house 'as a child'. And of course it also anticipates the ending of the relationship between Belle and Will at some unspecified – but presumably impending – occasion in the future. So a single hour has been plucked from at least twenty years, and maybe more.

Creative writers need to do this to focus the attention of their readers, listeners, audiences. The hour Robison has selected is a pivotal moment that allows us to see forwards and backwards in time. If Robison had elected to take us through all the events chronologically, she would have robbed the story of its power. She has *arranged* her story – has made a **plot** out of it – which enables her to reveal key details which contribute to the characterisation of the figures in it. The father's death comes to us as a surprise and also as a revelation about Belle and her mother's relationship, as we know Belle and her father have been close. It gives us a *contrast* – between the dancer and the accountant, between freedom and restraint.

This kind of editing or selection of the time-frame is vital in any genre. It mirrors the editing mentioned in Chapter 1, in which we noted that it is not necessary to depict every step of a journey. Creative writing is constantly about the twin processes of editing and arrangement. This is as true of novels, of creative non-fiction and drama as it is of the short story. You have to lead the reader or audience to moments and incidents which are most productive in revealing 'the whole story'.

---

## ACTIVITY

Think about arranging a piece of autobiographical life writing. Write down a list of pivotal moments in your life that you think would allow you to move backwards and forwards in time. Make some notes (or, better, draw a diagram), which shows what other points in time you are going to relate this to.

## DISCUSSION

My suspicion is that you will have come up with a range of options, which would be good. I hope they don't include the moment that you were born, not least because I suspect that you really won't remember it, even if you have been told about it! It is true that many celebrity autobiographies and biographies open with the phrase 'I was born in' – but unless you are a celebrity, in which case there might be some surprise factor, it is best to begin, or concentrate upon a particular event which allows you to describe a pivotal moment. The first memoir (so far) by Bob Dylan, *Chronicles: Volume One* (2004) opens with his signing to Columbia Records, which was indeed a pivotal moment for him. He invites us to think about how he came to this moment, what brought him there, and where it led. It is best if you begin with a startling, even uncharacteristic moment of your life so far: in that way, you invite speculation, and speculation is what intrigues a reader.

# Context and point of view

As I said at the outset of the chapter, an important context for your reader is going to be the standpoint from which you tell your story. We looked at the notion of perspective with the two contrasting news stories about the same event in the previous chapter. And of course, any story is told from one perspective rather than another. In Chapter 3, I mentioned first-person narrators and witness narrators (who are a species of first-person narrator).

## ACTIVITY

Write down a list of advantages and disadvantages of using a first-person narrator.

## DISCUSSION

I expect that you will have suggested that a first-person point-of-view is restricted only to what he, she (and on occasions, it) can see, and that this limited view means that your reader may get a poor understanding of other characters. (With an unreliable narrator, of course, this is the point: your reader understands better than your narrator.) Another disadvantage may be that the tone and pattern of the voice, even if it is varied, becomes tiresome. The single word 'I' is almost inevitably going to feature frequently. There are also going to be potential problems with any events which do not directly involve the narrator. Either these are going to have to be relayed to the narrator by other characters, either in person by a device such as a letter, both of which can be a clumsy process; or, they may have to be omitted. In other words, a first-person narrator has the potential to impede the action.

On the other hand, a first-person narrator offers your reader a more intimate experience, and it will also allow you to be more conversational in tone. You'll be able to loosen the vocabulary (if you want to). You'll be able to offer your reader an illusion of first-hand experience. In autobiographical life writing, of course, although it is possible to write about yourself in the third person, using the first person is pretty much a given. That's because the subject is you and your world. And in fiction, this may be equally the case: that the narrator is so central to the story – *is* the story, in effect – that writing from his or her standpoint is ideal. Short stories often lend themselves to the use of the first person. In a novel, you may need to consider the issue more carefully.

Notice, too, that prose writing is quite different from drama in this respect. In stage plays, it is very unusual to have a narrator of any sort, unless the play is a monologue. In Willy Russell's musical *Blood Brothers* (1985), there *is* a narrator, who comments on and interprets much of the action – to a certain degree, like a chorus in a Greek tragedy, offering their take on the action and characters to the audience. But it is rare to use this device in the theatre. In TV and radio plays, there are also examples of monologues, from Alan Bennett's *Talking Heads* (1988) to Lee Hall's *Spoonface Steinberg* (1997) – and the latter has subsequently been revised for the stage and for film. Monologues like this, however, are characteristically short (Bennett's monologues are about forty minutes long; Hall's is just under an hour). Practically all plays do not use first-person narrators: they show the audience what is taking place through the interaction of characters and events. Films sometimes use voiceovers, too, often at the outset: but a film is such an obviously visual medium that narration can be distracting.

We have already seen, however, that a first-person narration need not exclude other viewpoints. In 'Pretty Ice', Belle uses the first-person pronoun sixty-five times (not including in speech), and the story is between two and three thousand words long (relatively short for the genre). Hers, however, is not the only voice we hear, nor the only opinion. It is simply the dominant voice. Dialogue ensures that we hear from her mother, and, albeit briefly, from Will as well. If you look back at 'Pretty Ice', you will see that dialogue is the strongest weapon an author has to prevent a first-person narrator limiting your reader's experience. You'll also see how Robison uses her narrator and her conversations to give us key details of setting – like the abandoned dance hall on the icy morning.

---

The context of how the story is offered to your readers affects them very particularly. It affects their focus. There is another way of presenting a first-person narrator, one that blends his or her voice into the general narrative. In Chapter 5, there is an example of this, in the short passage discussing 'free indirect speech'. (To recap, free indirect speech is a technique whereby a character's voice is incorporated into the narrative voice itself. So the character's speech either to others or to him/herself is not set apart in quotation marks, but becomes interwoven with the narrative.) One of the best twentieth-century practitioners of this technique was Katherine Mansfield. This is the opening of her 1921 story, 'The Little Governess'.

Oh, dear, how she wished that it wasn't night-time. She'd have much rather travelled by day, much much rather. But the lady at the Governess Bureau said: 'You had better take an evening boat and then if you get into a compartment for Ladies Only in the train you will be far safer than sleeping in a foreign hotel. Don't go out of the carriage; don't walk about the corridors and *be sure* to lock the lavatory door if you go there. The train arrives at Munich at eight o'clock, and Frau Arnholdt says that the Hotel Grunewald is only one minute away. A porter can take you there. She will arrive at six the same evening, so you will have a nice quiet day to rest after the journey and rub up your German. And when you want anything to eat I would advise you to pop into the nearest baker's and get a bun and some coffee. You haven't been abroad before, have you?' 'No.' 'Well, I always tell my girls that it's better to mistrust people at first rather than trust them, and it's safer to suspect people of evil intentions rather than good ones. . . . It sounds rather hard but we've got to be women of the world, haven't we?'

It had been nice in the Ladies' Cabin. The stewardess was so kind and changed her money for her and tucked up her feet. She lay on one of the hard pink-sprigged couches and watched the other passengers, friendly and natural, pinning their hats to the bolsters, taking off their boots and skirts, opening dressing-cases and arranging mysterious rustling little packages, tying their heads up in veils before lying down. *Thud, thud, thud,* went the steady screw of the steamer. The stewardess pulled a green shade over the light and sat down by the stove, her skirt turned back over her knees, a long piece of knitting on her lap. On a shelf above her head there was a water-bottle with a tight bunch of flowers stuck in it. 'I like travelling very much,' thought the little governess. She smiled and yielded to the warm rocking.

But when the boat stopped and she went up on deck, her dress-basket in one hand, her rug and umbrella in the other, a cold, strange wind flew under her hat. She looked up at the masts and spars of the ship, black against a green glittering sky, and down to the dark landing-stage where strange muffled figures lounged, waiting; she moved forward with the sleepy flock, all knowing where to go to and what to do except her, and she felt afraid. Just a little – just enough to wish – oh, to wish that it was daytime and that one of those women who had smiled at her in the glass, when they both did their hair in the Ladies' Cabin, was somewhere near now. 'Tickets, please. Show your tickets. Have your tickets ready.' She went down the gangway balancing herself carefully on her heels. Then a man in a black leather cap came forward and touched her on the arm. 'Where for, Miss?' He spoke English – he must be a guard or a stationmaster with a cap like that. She had scarcely answered when he pounced on her dress-basket. 'This way,' he shouted, in a rude, determined voice, and elbowing his way he strode past the people. 'But I don't want a porter.' What a horrible man! 'I don't want a porter. I want to carry it myself.' She had to run to keep up with him, and her anger, far stronger than she, ran before her and snatched the bag out of the wretch's hand. He paid no attention at all, but swung on down the long dark platform, and across a railway line. 'He is a robber.' She was sure he was a robber as she stepped between the silvery rails and felt the cinders crunch under her shoes. On the other side – oh, thank goodness! – there was a train with Munich written on it. The man stopped by the huge lighted carriages. 'Second class?' asked the insolent voice. 'Yes, a Ladies' compartment.' She was quite out of breath. She opened her little purse to find something small enough to give this horrible man while he tossed her dress-basket into the rack of an empty carriage that had a ticket, *Dames Seules,* gummed on the window. She got into the train and handed him twenty centimes.

(Mansfield, 1920, pp. 239–41)

Immediately we can see that this is not written in the first person. We have a good external view of the governess – how she looks, how she talks, the setting in which Mansfield has placed her. More importantly, the rather scatty rhythm of the sentences, especially because of the way they are punctuated, precisely echoes the way the governess thinks and acts. Indeed, it is very much as if the governess is talking *to* us, despite the fact that it is not a first-person narrative.

Mansfield uses a variety of tactics to achieve this effect. She uses dialogue. She uses contrast. She tells us what the governess says out loud, gives us her opinion ('He is a robber.'). She tells us what the governess is thinking ('"I like travelling very much," thought the little governess') and she also shows her thoughts without needing to use the word 'thought' at all:

'But I don't want a porter.' *What a horrible man!* 'I don't want a porter. I want to carry it myself.' [my italics]

In this way, Mansfield interpolates phrases that indicate what is passing through the character's head, so that we know, from the vocabulary alone, that this is what she is feeling:

Oh, dear, how she wished that it wasn't night-time. She'd have much rather travelled by day, *much much rather.* [my italics]

111

On the other side – *oh, thank goodness!* – there was a train with Munich written on it. [my italics]

*Just a little – just enough to wish – oh, to wish that it was daytime* and that one of those women who had smiled at her in the glass, when they both did their hair in the Ladies' Cabin, was somewhere near now. [my italics]

This technique, as you can see, allows you to shuttle the reader between what a central character experiences, and what is going on around her. We have the advantage of being able to play the interior voice off against the exterior environment. The technique is not the same as Robison's in 'Pretty Ice', but the effect is the same. In each case we see a woman in the context of a narrative approach, each of which gives the reader setting and characterisation. The slightly arch and remote personality of Belle is depicted as clearly as the naïve, suspicious and flustered personality of the governess.

---

## ACTIVITY

I would now like you to try your hand at Mansfield's technique in *The Little Governess*. What you might like to try is to re-tell part of 'Pretty Ice' using Mansfield's approach, but equally, you might like to invent your own character, and try a short opening to a story (around 300 to 400 words) with a character of your own invention. The best way to begin is to choose two character-defining adjectives for your central figure. You can select your own, but here are some possibilities:

boisterous, angry, pensive, pedantic, lethargic, perplexed, hesitant, complacent, intense, gloomy, excitable

## DISCUSSION

You may have found that the exercise was quite taxing, in that Mansfield shifts so quickly from exterior to interior views. Perhaps the hardest thing to manage is the rhythm of the sentences. In Chapter 3, we noted that a voice's rhythm is important, when looking at the extract from H.G. Wells's *Tono-Bungay*. In Chapter 5, we stressed the importance of variety of sentence-length. If you look at each of the passages – Wells, Robison, Mansfield – you will see that punctuation is helping to control the pace. It's worth having a look back over what you've written, and seeing if adding or subtracting punctuation, or changing sentence-lengths, will improve what you've written.

But what if you don't want to write from a character's point of view? What if you don't want one character to be the main focus? Who then is telling the story, and how can it be told? The next section explores this further.

## Telling a story

For much of the time in this chapter, and in earlier ones too, we have focused on a character narrating a story. Yet of course, this isn't quite correct. As a writer, you are really the person who is narrating the story, and your choice (let us say) of a first-person speaker, is your own narrative tactic. In some novels, notably in the nineteenth century, this reminder that the writer was in control could be made quite clear. At the end the first chapter of George Eliot's second novel, *The Mill on the Floss* (1860), she writes:

> Ah, my arms are really benumbed. I have been pressing my elbows on the arms of my chair, and dreaming that I was standing on the bridge in front of Dorlcote Mill, as it looked one February afternoon many years ago. Before I dozed off, I was going to tell you what Mr. and Mrs. Tulliver were talking about, as they sat by the bright fire in the left-hand parlor, on that very afternoon I have been dreaming of.
>
> (Eliot, 1960 [1860], p. 13)

It is also Eliot's habit occasionally to pass judgement on her characters during the course of the novel. If we want, we can go one stage further back, and argue that Eliot has created a version of herself (the 'I' in the paragraph above) to tell the story, because after all, it's presumably a fiction that she dozed off; and she certainly doesn't know 'you' personally.

Whether you want to argue that the 'I' is George Eliot, or a version of herself, this ostentatious reference to being the storyteller is relatively rare today, other than in those novels that like to write with irony and erudition about the narrative process while constructing a narrative, for example Italo Calvino's *If on a Winter's Night a Traveller* (1979). I enjoy fictions like this, and they have had a profound influence on how novels and short stories are studied, but for the sake of directness, I am focusing on the construction of story.

As a fiction writer, you have two main choices if you decide that you don't want to use a first-person narrator, and the choice you make will affect the way that what you write is read – it will change its context, as noted at the start of this chapter. You can opt to tell a story as if you know everything (you are therefore creating an invisible 'omniscient' narrator, who makes no reference to the act of narration, and who operates rather like a film camera). A parallel to this is telling a story as if you know nothing at all, in which case, you are going to be reliant on letting all the events speak for themselves: put simply, you won't be able to write 'meanwhile, a few miles away', or anything remotely similar.

Or you can tell a story but restrict the focus and awareness of events to a greater or lesser degree to a particular individual, most probably your main one. In this case, you are once again keeping your awareness of the fact that you're the storyteller quiet. You are siding with your chosen character – perhaps for the whole piece, or perhaps moving from one character in one scene to another character in another scene.

If you apply this to 'Pretty Ice', it would work out as follows. A narrator who knew everything would be able, in the third person, to present us with Belle, and to describe the impact on her of the arrival of Will at the station.

> She knew when she saw him that it would be the last time that they met, and that they would never be married. Her mother was oblivious, and chattered gamely to the new arrival. In the distance, a lonely skater showed off his skill.

And so on, although of course there would be dialogue. A narrator who knew nothing (that is, pretended to, as the narrator is the writer) wouldn't be able to tell what Belle was thinking, so it might be something more like:

> Will greeted Belle with a kiss; she looked at his gold-rimmed spectacles, quizzically. When they got to her mother's car, which she had parked in an empty cab lane, he tossed away the coffee-cup. 'Does your mom smoke?' he said.

All we have here are snatches of fact. If we have read the original, we will understand exactly what 'quizzically' means – 'doubtfully'. But if this is a reader's first encounter, he or she will have to do a great deal more work to interpret what is going on. Narrators who know 'nothing' rely on readers to understand the very slightest nuance. It means that everything must be shown, and the effect is often that there is more dialogue.

However, if we limit the viewpoint to one character, and Belle is the obvious choice, then the result will be very similar to the original, which is of course seen directly from Belle's point of view. It would be comparatively easy to turn 'Pretty Ice' into the third person, without disturbing very much of the action. It would still be a good story. But it would lose that edge and tension that come from Belle's insecurity, as offered to us in the first person:

> I didn't want to see how my face and hair looked after a night of accounting.
>
> I wished he had freshened up and put on a better shirt before leaving the train.
>
> I was trying for a clean center-part in my hair.

In a longer piece, however, a reader might well appreciate a break from Belle's often self-regarding, but frustrated view of the world as a musicologist who has wound up in accountancy. As a writer, you would be able, in a different scene, to look at the world from Will's tediously botanical point of view ('A lot of shrubs damaged and turn brown, and the trees don't blossom right').

The context changes with the method of narration, then. As an author, you have many choices to make about how you tell a story, and the length of the story might well be an important contextual issue. It is important to add that there are other options. A narrative that shifted the viewpoint from scene to scene, whether in the first or third person, might refresh itself. There are many novels, and some plays, that offer you an alternative and contradictory view of the same events. There are novels like William Faulkner's *As I Lay Dying* (1930), that uses fifteen narrators, and Graham Swift's *Last Orders* (1996) (eight narrators) which borrows from and expertly recalibrates Faulkner's novel by shifting the location from Mississippi to London and Margate.

These examples look like templates for any aspiring writer. They aren't. Looking at events through different sets of eyes can enhance what you write, but starting with the idea that any number of voices can chip in as the narrator is a recipe for disaster. Even a shift of third-person viewpoint from one person to another in a short story can cause a reader unnecessary confusion. The same goes for non-human narrators. For instance, I can think of several stories and novels partly or wholly narrated by dogs: Paul Auster's *Timbuktu* (1999), Georgi Vladimov's *Faithful Ruslan* (1975), Franz Kafka's *Investigations of a Dog* (1922), Jack London's *White Fang* (1903), Virginia Woolf's *Flush, a Biography* (1933). They are *tours-de-force*; but they are not exemplars. The same goes for novels and stories narrated by young children – very, very hard to do, because of the problem of vocabulary. If you are beginning to write, it is best to begin with the experience with which you are familiar: being (an adult) human. The context for a short story is that it is *short*. That means restricting place, time, and number of characters: 'Pretty Ice' gives you three, four if you include Belle's father. As with a scene in a drama, in whatever medium, the fewer characters you are developing, the more likely you are to be successful. And in conclusion it is worth remembering that the ultimate context for writing is not genre, point of view, or the use of time, but remembering that you have readers. It doesn't matter if they are flicking pages, navigating a Kindle, reading your work online, watching your work on a stage, hearing your work in an audio-book or on the radio, or watching your work on a television or in a cinema. Your main context is your audience, and your need to grip them and to make them want to read on.

# 8  'Literary' language

## Defining 'literature'

In the Language Studies chapters so far we've looked at language use from a variety of different contexts: everyday speech and writing, newspaper articles and television programmes, plays and novels. We've considered differences in structure between spoken and written discourse, between standard and non-standard dialects, and we've looked at how 'genres' of communication exist in everyday contexts such as the job interview. In this chapter we ask if there's anything specific about the way language is used in literature. Is there a distinct category of 'literary language'? Or, to put it another way, can we explain what counts as literature in linguistic terms?

There are a number of different ways to approach this issue of what counts as literature. The French theorist Roland Barthes remarked that literature is simply 'what gets taught' (cited in Eagleton, 1983, p. 197). In other words, if something is put on the curriculum at school or university, it thereby has the status of 'literature' bestowed upon it. This is obviously a rather flippant remark, but it does point to the way in which society's beliefs and opinions play a part in determining what is valued as literature. The linguist Paul Simpson makes a similar point when he says that the 'property of "literariness" is not an immutable or permanent quality of language. It is not something that texts are; rather, it is something conferred upon them according to what they do' (Simpson, 1997, p. 8). And yet, one aspect of literariness would, intuitively, seem to relate to the use of language. Literary writers are those who manipulate language in particular – and often particularly creative – ways. They fashion and shape the same resource that we all use in everyday life into something distinctive, arresting, engaging and artful.

## Literary stylistics

A key approach to the analysis of literature from a linguistic point of view is what is known as **stylistics**. As the term suggests, stylistics is the study of style in language. Style, in this context, refers to the choices people make about their language use, and how these choices create a distinctive manner of expression. There are different approaches that stylistics can take to this topic, but one of the most prominent strategies is to look at the way in which style is an intrinsic element of the text itself. That's to say, a reader's appreciation of the style – and of how it creates an aesthetic, artistic or distinctive effect – relates to the way the text is organised. It relates to the choice and combination of words, to how the vocabulary and grammar are arranged so as to produce these particular effects. This approach focuses mainly on the *form* of the language used (the look and sound of the words, and the patterns made by their combination), and is therefore referred to as a 'formalist' approach.

One the most influential formalist approaches to the linguistic study of literature is that developed in the early part of the twentieth century by scholars in Russia. This group, known as the 'Russian Formalists', suggested that a key factor of what makes a piece of writing literary is that it draws attention to the use of language itself. That's to say, a literary effect comes from the explicit creative manipulation of the linguistic resources being used. And this is achieved by deviating from the way that normal speech or everyday writing is constructed, and by 'foregrounding' some property of the language itself. The result is what the Russian Formalists referred to as a process of defamiliarisation, or 'making strange': through the manipulation of language the writer is able to make the reader freshly appreciate the subject of the text, and thus see the world in a new light.

Literary stylistics therefore looks at deviations from normative language use (i.e. away from the speech patterns of everyday life) and at the patterning created by the writer's use of language in a text. It looks at how the use of repetitions or juxtapositions in the sounds and shapes of the language produce effects such as rhyme and rhythm, and how the relationship between choice of word and the construction of meaning can augment an everyday understanding of the scenarios or experiences the text addresses. In the rest of this chapter we'll have a brief look at an example of this type of analysis. We'll then go on in the next chapter to consider the process in more detail by looking at it from the viewpoint of the writer rather than analyst, and investigate the ways in which playing with the patterning of language can create poetic voices.

# Foregrounding

### ACTIVITY

Have a look at William Blake's poem 'London' below. This was published in his collection *Songs of Experience* in 1794. While you are reading it, look out for the ways that the choice and arrangement of the language create certain patterns in the text, which are different from the flow of everyday speech. What are the effects of this patterning?

I wander thro' each charter'd street,
Near where the charter'd Thames does flow,
And mark in every face I meet
Marks of weakness, marks of woe.

In every cry of every Man,
In every Infant's cry of fear,
In every voice, in every ban,
The mind-forg'd manacles I hear.

How the Chimney-sweeper's cry
Every black'ning Church appalls;
And the hapless Soldier's sigh
Runs in blood down Palace walls.

But most thro' midnight streets I hear
How the youthful Harlot's curse
Blasts the new born Infant's tear,
And blights with plagues the Marriage hearse.
                    (1967 [1789/1794])


## DISCUSSION

One of the ways in which this poem foregrounds the language it uses – and plays on the form and combination of the words – is through its use of rhythm. Rhythm in poetry is created by means of patterns of stress in the pronunciation of words. If you read the lines aloud you will get a sense of where the stress falls in each word and phrase, and how this is repeated from line to line. Although everyday speech also has a rhythm, it is not as pronounced or distinctive as verse. Another aspect of the patterning is rhyme, which exploits the aural similarity of words. Rhyme is what one might call a phonetic echo, and again, as it reoccurs across the poem, it sets up expectations in the reader that can either be fulfilled (when the pattern continues in a regular way) or thwarted (when it shifts or is abandoned).

We'll look closely at the dynamics of both rhythm and rhyme in the next chapter; but for the moment we can simply note the way they both work here to create a sense of regularity, of forward movement, and maybe even inevitability. Alternate lines in each stanza rhyme, and the rhythm moves along with a pronounced and steady beat. In a sense, the rhythm echoes the act of wandering, pace after pace, through the streets of London. The sound of the poem therefore parallels the subject it deals with, and in this way contributes to its meaning. So once again, *how* something is expressed becomes an important complement to what is being expressed.

The steady repetition of rhyming words at the end of each alternate line is matched by several other sorts of repetition. One is the simple reuse of words from line to line. In the first stanza, for example, *charter'd* is prominently repeated in both the first and second lines, as are *mark* and *marks* in the next two. The repetition in this latter case involves a subtle shift – in the third line the word is used as a verb, while in the fourth it reappears as a noun. So Blake is here playing on the multiple meanings of the same form of a word; and in doing so he links the perspective of the narrator (the way he 'marks' or notices things) with the physical and emotional properties of what he's looking at ('Marks of weakness' etc.).

Another aspect of the sound of the words that is noticeable in the poem is **alliteration**: the repetition of consonants, particularly at the beginning of words. For example, in that phrase 'Marks of weakness, marks of woe', not only is the word *marks* repeated, but so is the *w*-sound in *weakness* and *woe*. The phrase also uses grammatical patterning, with the two noun phrases ('Marks of weakness' and 'marks of woe') paralleling each other in structure. So within those six words, there is a very neatly orchestrated patterning of linguistic forms.

Another aspect of language which Blake manipulates in creative ways is the meaning of the words and phrases. The use of **similes** and **metaphors** to compare things is a common technique in poetry, and is especially effective for making the reader perceive a concept or scenario in a new light. One of the most arresting metaphors in this poem is 'mind-forg'd manacles', in which people's beliefs or ways of thinking are likened to physical shackles. There are other notable juxtapositions of meaning as well, such as the notion of the 'Marriage hearse', in which two concepts which are conventionally thought of as quite distinct, possibly even opposed to each other, are brought together to provide an enigmatic image.

---

There is a lot more to literature than just the ways in which it manipulates the formal properties of language, of course. We have not discussed the overall subject or themes of the poem at all, nor have we mentioned the historical context in which Blake's poem was written - the fact that it was composed at a time of great social upheaval, with the aftermath of the French Revolution shaping political and personal experiences across Europe. All we've done is highlight some of the rhetorical devices at play within the text, and how they work from a linguistic point of view. But certainly one element of much literary language is the way that it draws attention to itself by using these sorts of rhetorical devices - by focusing on the sounds, the grammar, and the meaning - and in doing so, it can surprise the reader into a fresh perception, appreciation of and response to the subject matter. In the next chapter we'll continue looking at these strategies, and delve in more detail into the practices of poetic composition.

# 9 Writing poetry

## The meaning of 'poetic'

So far we have looked at every genre of creative writing, except poetry. In this final chapter we will be looking at how to create a 'poetic' voice, and how to create a poem. The difference between the voices and texts in the earlier chapters and the ones you will encounter and invent in this chapter is that the voices here are consciously 'unreal', which is to say that they are seeking to go, self-consciously, beyond the mimicry of real-life voices. But first, let's define our terms.

---

### ACTIVITY

In the previous chapter we discussed the slippery nature of the terms 'literary' and 'literature'. Now take a moment to think about what you understand by the words 'poetic' and 'poem'. Do the two words mean the same thing? Once you have considered this, read the extracts below. All three are experimental prose. How might they be said to be 'poetic'?

1. The boys are dreaming wicked or of the bucking ranches of the night and the jollyrodgered sea. And the anthracite statues of the horses sleep in the fields, and the cows in the byres, and the dogs in the wet-nosed yard; and the cats nap in the slant corners or lope sly, streaking and needling, on the one cloud of the roofs.

2. he was called
   Plato Aristotle Copernicus Galileo
   Bacon Descartes Newton
   and because he was so interested in clocks he began to take apart other clocks
      man clocks woman clocks animal clocks plant
      clocks so soon his home was littered and strewn
   with pieces
   of the different clocks
   and the odd thing was

the more he took the clocks apart
with his sharp instruments
the less they seemed to work
the less they ticked
the stiller the cogs and wheels
were ...

3. frseeeeeeeefronnnng train somewhere whistling the strength those engines have in them like big giants and the water rolling all over and out of them all sides like the end of Loves old sweeeetsonnnng the poor men that have to be out all the night from their wives and families in those roasting engines stifling it was today Im glad I burned the half of those old Freemans and Photo Bits leaving things like that lying about hes getting very careless and threw the rest of them up in the WC Ill get him to cut them tomorrow for me instead of having them there for the next year to get a few pence for them have him asking wheres last Januarys paper and all those old overcoats I bundled out of the hall making the place hotter than it is that rain was lovely and refreshing just after my beauty sleep I thought it was going to get like Gibraltar my goodness the heat there before the levanter came on black as night and the glare of the rock standing up in it like a big giant compared with their 3 Rock mountain they think is so great with the red sentries here and there the poplars and they all whitehot and the smell of the rainwater in those tanks watching the sun all the time weltering down on you faded all that lovely frock fathers friend Mrs Stanhope sent me from the B Marche paris what a shame

## DISCUSSION

'Poetic' can mean, simply enough, that language is written in poetic form, and it is on this sense of 'poetic' that this chapter will mainly concentrate. The word 'poetic' can also be used as a compliment, almost as a synonym for 'moving'. It can mean, equally simply, 'using language creatively' – the sense in which David Mamet uses it in Chapter 3 of this book. However, 'poetic' can also be used to suggest a rich, perhaps even elaborate language, a language that depends much more than everyday speech on overt metaphor and simile. By implication there is something self-conscious about this kind of 'poetic' voice, which is by no means confined to poetry. There are many examples of prose writers and indeed dramatists who use a rich, intense vocabulary, 'foregrounding' the language itself (as was discussed in the previous chapter), or writing in a way that celebrates language as art almost more than as communication.

The three extracts above are taken respectively from: a radio play by Dylan Thomas, a stage play by Bryony Lavery, and an extract from Molly Bloom's soliloquy in the closing section of James Joyce's novel *Ulysses* (1922). Each uses language in a way that might be called unusual, perhaps eccentric, and in a more intense way than we would associate with more conventional prose. The writing is consciously straining at the boundaries of what is expected – either by coining words, or by running words together or punctuating (with line breaks in Lavery's case) in an unusual manner, or dispensing with punctuation entirely. There is, in each case, a heightened sense of language as something more mobile and fluent than we might find in everyday conversation.

The voices in all three extracts are super-distinctive. In a note to another play, *A Wedding Story* (2000), Lavery is explicit about her unusual uses of language, which she describes as 'deliberate eccentricities' to help actors with the subtext:

> This play is laid out to help the actors find
> the true rhythms of dramatic speech.
>
> None of the characters speak in sentences
> or observe punctuation or breathe at the right time.
>
> Because          often
> They are in           torment.
> (Lavery, 2007, p. 6)

In defining 'poem' in the previous activity, you may have written something about its shape or layout. If you open any book of poetry, the first thing you will see is that the lines have been arranged in some way. You will see more white space on the page than is usual for a page of prose fiction, and you will sense that there is some structure or form. The shape on the page is very much part of the genre.

You may see the poem laid out in **stanzas**, you may see the poem set out in lines of roughly similar length or you may see the poem experimenting with lines of different length. It is hard to imagine a poem that does not look like a poem. However, this won't do as a definition, since you could easily rearrange a passage of prose to resemble a poem.

What you will not see straight away, unless the poem is using a traditional rhyme scheme, is the importance to a poem of repetition, which we touched on in the previous chapter. Rhyme itself, incidentally, comes in many forms, and some of them are not instantly visible. The box on rhyme explains the many ways in which the word 'rhyme' can be applied.

## Rhyme

There are many different forms of rhyme, of which the most well known is end-rhyme which (as the term suggests) occurs at the end of the line. An exact rhyme (e.g. 'bend'/'send' or 'wind'/'pinned') is called 'full rhyme'. A rhyme scheme can be notated by using letters, e.g. *abcb* would mean that the second line rhymed with the fourth, and that the other two lines did not rhyme. William Blake's 'London' has an *abab cdcd* etc. scheme with full rhymes.

Half-rhyme, sometimes also called 'slant rhyme', is when the end-words are approximately the same – most often the consonants are the same, but the vowel between them is varied: so for instance 'main'/'mean', 'filling'/'falling' are half-rhymes. There are two good uses to which half-rhyme can be put: the inexactness of the rhyme can help create a mood of dissonance, of uncertainty. Half-rhymes can also quieten a poem: exact rhymes can make a poem more assertive, while half-rhymes can be used to tone down that directness.

Near-rhyme is when the final words are similar, so that there is the suggestion of rhyme, no more – as when a stanza in the poem 'Considering the Snail' by Thom Gunn uses the end-words 'stirring', 'tell', 'there', 'nothing', 'all', 'later'. The rhyme-scheme here is *abcabc*, but the *a* rhyme is only in the echo of the unstressed syllable *–ing* in 'stirring' and 'nothing'; the *b* rhyme is a half-rhyme (*tell/all*); and the *c* rhyme connects a stressed syllable (*there*) with an unstressed syllable (*-er*). This kind of almost invisible rhyming can give a poem a surprising sense of structure.

Internal rhyme is when words within one line, or in one line and in another, or in one line and at the end of another, match each other as full end-rhyme does. I use it in a poem called 'Take It Away', based on a mother who said just that to the midwife after her first child was born. (It struck me that this is what bandleaders sometimes said to musicians when a jazzy tune was about to begin.)

> No-one *heard* (and she'd never remember)
> that moment when they stuffed
> the new child on her breast,
> how, hearing the *blur*, the ab*surd*
> image of Joe Loss oc*curr*ed to *her*
> (Greenwell, 2006, p. 55)

At first sight, this might look like an unrhymed poem, but the *–ur* sound is present five times in this stanza. And there is a buried full-rhyme – *heard/absurd/occurred*. It's just that only one of them turns up at the end of a line – *absurd*. I was avoiding the exactness of end-rhyme – to avoid the assertiveness of it, as mentioned above.

Just as there can be full internal rhyme, there can also be half-rhyme buried in a line, or a sequence of similar sounds, particularly vowel sounds. Consonantal echoes can make a poem too obvious, and need to be used sparingly.

## Repetition and poetry

When you create a poem, you are consciously shaping language, more consciously, I would argue, than if you are shaping any prose, even the experimentally 'poetic' prose above. And the most important method used by poets to shape language is repetition.

There are three particular ways in which the writing of poetry can use repetition. One is the repetition of some formal aspect of structure, such as the use of a pattern of stanzas (sometimes called **verses**, although 'verse' is more commonly now used to define a section of a song). Another is the repetition, either exactly or less precisely, of a phrase. A third and perhaps most important device is the repetition of sounds – either of vowels or of consonants – which may happen across the length of a poem or at specific intervals. The repetition of sounds is affected by where the beat of a line falls – if the beat falls on similar sounds, it is more noticeable. So, for instance, in my poem 'The Muse's Blues', the beat falls in the following lines on two short *i* sounds ('*i*rritates'/'l*i*ps'), two short *a* sounds ('fr*a*nks'/'*a*ngry') and three long *e* sounds ('t*ee*th'/'*e*vening'/'sl*ee*ps'):

> She irritates her lips,
> and franks his message with angry teeth.
> That evening, she sleeps like an ocean.
> (Greenwell, 2006, p. 94)

There is another short *i* sound ('w*i*th'); two other short *a* sounds ('*a*nd' and '*a*n'); and another pair of long *e* sounds ('Sh*e*' and 'sh*e*'), but they aren't doing the work – because the beat does not fall on them.

Of course, poets do not write by thinking up sound-patterns and then grafting subjects on to them. However, in successive drafts of poems, the kinds of amendments that poets make are frequently to do with adjusting the pattern of sound and other repetitions so that they are appropriate. It is a good idea therefore to be clear about the ways in which vowels and consonants, syllables and stresses, and different kinds of rhyme might work. You might find this quite technical, but my approach here is to give you some of the detail about the way sound works, before approaching the idea of creating poems. Many people are anxious about creating poems, and so having a sense of the mechanics should help demystify the process.

## Vowels

The vowels in English are *a, e, i, o, u*, and sometimes also y (which is a consonant or vowel depending on its context). They are the sounds made by breath through the larynx and mouth that do not use the tongue, lips or teeth. As noted in Chapter 2 of this book, the relationship between the alphabet and speech sounds is not straightforward, and so sociolinguists will use a specialised alphabet such as the IPA when they wish to describe speech in a detailed and accurate way. What I am giving you here, though, is a lay guide to speech sounds, which is sufficient for our present purposes. Vowels can be either long or short, and spelling alone will not show this. A short vowel sound would include:

| | |
|---|---|
| *a* | as in 'can' |
| *e* | as in 'bed' |
| *i* | as in 'tin' |
| *o* | as in 'hot' |
| *u* | as in 'crumb' |
| *y* | as in 'pyramid' or 'handy' (note the difference). |

A long vowel sound would include:

| | |
|---|---|
| *a* | as in 'fate' |
| *e* | as in 'swede' |
| *i* | as in 'time' |
| *o* | as in 'hotel' |
| *u* | as in 'flute' or 'duty' (note the difference) |
| *y* | as in 'why' |

However, there are many other ways of combining vowels to create a longer sound – 'aardvark', 'beet', 'wool', 'spool', 'Caesar', 'weight', 'believe', 'waif', 'gaol', 'caul', 'Teutonic', 'foal', 'spoil', 'mouth', 'four', 'tough', 'tuile', 'beautiful'. These vowel sounds correspond to items in the list above. There are also many instances of vowels that are changed by the (usually silent, depending on your dialect) consonant succeeding them: 'hard', 'birth', 'hearth', 'spur', and so on. The repetition of a vowel sound is called **assonance**.

## Consonants

The English alphabet gives us twenty-one consonants, including *y*. However, some of the alphabetical sounds are duplicates, as with the 'soft' *c* of 'dice' and the 'hard' *c* of 'biscuit', which are respectively duplicated by *s* and *k*. And there are sounds simply not represented in the alphabet, including both 'hard' and 'soft' versions of *th* (as in 'this' and 'youth'), each of which had separate symbols in Old English. Many consonants are no longer sounded, as with the *k* in 'knot', and there are subtle other differences, such as the sound of *g* after an *n*, as in 'sing' and 'longer'.

There are of course many combinations of consonants – if you take a common word such as 'strength', there are six successive consonantal sounds (*s, t, r, n, g, th*). That means the word takes longer to say than a word with fewer consonants, or to 'hear' when reading. That will slow a line down. Writers do not sit and count consonants – but it is a good idea to be aware of their potential effect. Some consonants are also invariably 'hard' and others 'soft', but this does depend on frequency and context. Certainly the consonantal sounds *d, k, t* are harder, just as the consonantal sounds *f, l, m, r* and *s* are generally softer. There is a particular word for the repetition of an *s* sound – sibilance.

Consonants can thin or thicken a line, causing it to accelerate or decelerate, just as they can make it more or less aggressive, or more or less gentle in sound. As we saw in the previous chapter, the repetition of a consonantal sound is called alliteration.

## ACTIVITY

Before you tackle the main part of this activity, read the box on vowels and consonants as many times as you need to, in order to absorb the information fully before moving on to the second part of the activity. You may find it helpful to read aloud the words given as examples.

I'm now going to ask you to experiment. What you write does not have to make perfect sense. You can even see the activity as an exercise in pure sound. Below is an opening phrase. I want you to create a pair of lines continuing from the phrase, in which there is some form of repetition, either of a vowel or consonant – as much repetition as you like. You can rhyme the pair of lines if you like, but it's not necessary.

It's time to catch …

## DISCUSSION

It would have been fine if your lines were nonsensical, perhaps as follows:

> It's time to catch the accidental patch, to climb
> the hat-stand while the crimes are watched and tied.

Or you might quite reasonably have made sense with your lines, as in:

> It's time to catch a final glimpse of you,
> and naturally I'm trying to keep track.

I am not suggesting that this kind of forced patterning will lead you easily to a poem. It is a limbering-up exercise, and what I have been trying to do here is to concentrate almost entirely on echoing the *ti-*, or *t* or *-ime* sounds in 'time', and the *-at/-atch* sound in 'catch'. In the nonsense version, it is of course easier: 'time'/'climb'/'crimes'/'tied' and 'catch'/'patch'/'hat'/'watch'. (Notice that 'watch' is a half-rhyme.) In the second attempt, I have 'time'/'final'/'I'm'/'track', and 'catch'/'nat-'/'track'. I have included 'track' twice because it echoes the *t* of 'time' and the short *a* of 'catch'.

In the discussion above, rather artificially, I have constructed a brief pattern of repetitions, which we might call 'harmonies'. In the next section, I will look at how a song lyric and a poem use echoes like this to construct their poetic voices.

---

# Poetry and song

Poetry is a lineal descendant of song. In a pre-literate age, a song would need to have possessed the essential qualities required for being committed to memory – that is, a great deal of repetition, including the use of refrains. (Homer's *Iliad*, one of the oldest extant poems, is full of repetitions.) The Welsh word *cerdd* means both 'song' and 'poem', and 'sonnet' comes from the Italian word for 'little song', *sonetto*.

Songs continue to be repetitive, to use (for instance) choruses. Poetry has developed from being spoken to being written (although, of course, poems continue to be read aloud, to be recited or performed). As they have developed, the repetitions and echoes they use have become more subtle. In contemporary poetry – much of which continues to use rhyme – the repetitions that give the poem its voice are more deeply buried in the text. What gives a poem its distinctive flavour is often its repetition not just of words but of sounds, in particular the sounds of vowels. In effect, poems become like echo-chambers.

In the next activity you will look at two readings, both of which explore a sense of separation. One of them is the opening of a relatively contemporary song, 'Amelia' by Joni Mitchell, and the other is a contemporary poem, 'Golf' by Jane Draycott. Mitchell's song is addressed to Amelia Earhart, the adventurous airwoman of the 1920s and 1930s, with whom the voice identifies. Draycott's poem opens with the idea of golfers being always 'one step ahead', and develops the idea into a deeper sense of the separation between one group of people and another, into perhaps the separation between the present and the past.

---

## ACTIVITY

Read the extract from Joni Mitchell's song 'Amelia' and Jane Draycott's poem 'Golf'. What repetitions and echoes can you find in each?

### from **Amelia**

I was driving across the burning desert
When I spotted six jet planes
Leaving six white vapor trails across the bleak terrain
It was the hexagram of the heavens
It was the strings of my guitar
Amelia, it was just a false alarm

The drone of flying engines
Is a song so wild and blue
It scrambles time and seasons if it gets through to you
Then your life becomes a travelogue
Of picture-post-card-charms
Amelia, it was just a false alarm

(Mitchell, 1997, p. 158)

### **Golf**

In the mirage we saw three figures, kings
perhaps or the type with the migrant gene –
adventurous, always one step ahead
striking a path through the desert simply
by instinct, first to smell the oasis,
first then to gaze on the moon in the well.
We struck out towards them. It felt as if
boundless and bare the morning might take us

and carry us elsewhere, somewhere ahead
which wasn't a carpet of dandelions
struck by the clock of the wind again and again
and no one to blame but yourself.
Between us and the men who looked like us
a river, an ocean of sand, a gulf.

(Draycott, 2009, p. 47)

## DISCUSSION

The repetitions in Mitchell's song are predictably more obvious *because* it is a song. There is a refrain ('Amelia, it was just a false alarm'); there are several examples of rhyme or near-rhyme: 'planes'/'terrain', 'guitar'/'alarm', 'blue'/'you', 'charms'/'alarm'. There are also several internal echoes: 'across'/'spotted', 'vapor tra*i*ls', 'fly'/'wild'/'time', '*hex*agram'/'*heav*ens', 'drone'/'so', 'eng*ines*'/'seas*ons*', 'thr*ough*'/'y*ou*'. And a key phrase is repeated too: 'It was'/'it was'/'it was'/'it was'/'it was'. Not only that, the words 'Amelia' and 'alarm' both use the same two key consonants, *m* and *l*. And an interesting echo, which you will hear if you listen to the song, 'false'/'alarm', comes from Mitchell's Canadian pronunciation, and is an example of the regional variation that we discussed in Chapter 2.

The repetitions in 'Amelia' not only make the song easier to remember, but also to sing. In Draycott's poem, however, there are just as many repetitions and echoes, less obvious at first, and principally of vowel-sounds: 'f*i*gures'/'k*i*ngs', 't*y*pe'/'m*i*grant', 'adventur*ous*'/'step'/'ahead', 's*i*mply'/'*i*nstinct', '*oa*sis'/'g*a*ze', 'w*e*ll'/'f*e*lt', 'b*ou*ndless'/'b*a*re', 'b*a*re'/'some*where*', 'else*where*'/'ah*ead*', 'str*u*ck'/'cl*o*ck', 'ag*ai*n'/'bl*a*me', '*u*s'/'g*u*lf'. There are repetitions, too, of words: 'first to'/'first then to', 'strike'/'struck'/'struck', 'ahead'/'ahead', 'again'/'again'. She also half-rhymes the title with the final word.

To put it another way, the pattern of harmonies in Draycott's poem is more intricate than in Mitchell's song, although both of them have patterns of echo and repetition. Draycott's poem has also cunningly borrowed the phrase 'boundless and bare' from Percy Bysshe Shelley's 'Ozymandias' (1818), a poem set in a desert, and about a confrontation between a bewildered onlooker and a wrecked and ancient memorial plinth: emphasising the distance between present and past.

What creates the poetic voice – what marks it out – is the attention to what we might call the melody of words. This is not to suggest that a writer obsesses over every echo – sometimes echoes occur naturally in the writing, in the discovery of the subject and mood. But the drafting process in each case will have woven the echoes in more securely. Nor is it to suggest that every song or poem contains such a proliferation of echoes and repetitions. But it is to underline the way in which a poetic voice distinguishes itself from the everyday voice by the use of such devices.

---

You may be familiar with some of the technical terms used to describe the patterns of lines in metric poetry (for instance 'iambic pentameter'). There are many technical terms, and they can be baffling if you are attempting to compose poetry.

It is important, however, to know the difference between a stressed syllable and an unstressed syllable, because a writer uses the syllables on which the beat or stress falls to create both rhythmic and harmonic patterns. Although there are some slight regional variations, the stress pattern of any word is quite easy to work out. The word 'father' is pronounced with the stress on the first syllable – *fa*ther. The word 'across' is pronounced with the stress on the second syllable – a*cross*. The word 'frightening' has a stress on the first syllable – *fright*ening. Sometimes the strength of the stress on a syllable can be affected by the place it occupies in a line: you can only really work this out by reading it aloud.

So, for instance, in my sequence 'Speechless', one section runs as follows:

> If my father's face had had jam on it,
> I should have licked it away.
>
> But it's clean-cold, and I examine it,
> and kiss it. I say
>
> *You poor old bugger.* He merely gurns,
> his teeth out. The shop-bell sing
>
> and I breathe the lilies and the ferns,
> held in this cell.
> (Greenwell, 2011, p. 86)

I would say that the stresses in the first four lines fall, perhaps with slightly different weight, on the emboldened syllables below:

> If my **fa**ther's **face** had had **jam** on it,
> I should have **licked** it a**way**.
>
> But it's **clean-cold**, and I ex**am**ine it,
> and **kiss** it.

The word I have left open to doubt is 'should'. Its principal meaning here is that 'it would have been my response'; but I can see that readers might choose the second implication, which is that 'it would have been my obligation, one which I would have failed'. So I wouldn't blame anyone for placing a stress on 'should'. When I read this poem aloud, I make the firm beat fall on 'licked'.

Even if locating the pattern of stress is sometimes a slightly inexact art, developing a sense of the rise and fall, and an idea of the pattern of emphatic and weaker syllables, is important for the creator of a poetic voice. Poetry is more musical than most prose – because, as I've noted, its ancestry is in song or in chant. Aristotle wrote in his *Poetics* of 'melody and rhythm' being 'natural' to humans, and poetry makes the most of that tendency (1996, p. 7). In fact, he viewed it as so natural that he advised orators to make sure they didn't become overly metrical.

The best way to learn about syllables is to try writing in 'syllabics'. There are no rules about line length other than that each successive stanza has to have the same number of syllables in the corresponding lines (e.g. if line 2 has nine syllables in the first stanza, line 2 in the second and further stanzas has to have nine syllables as well). Dylan Thomas was perhaps the most interesting exponent of this in the last hundred years. One of his poems, 'Over Sir John's Hill' has five stanzas each of which follows this syllable pattern: 5, 6, 13, 5, 1, 14, 4, 14, 4, 14, 13. But he also wrote 'In My Craft or Sullen Art', in which *all* the lines have seven syllables.

If there is one rule – *convention* would be a better word – it's that you do not split a word across a line (otherwise, why write in syllabics, if you think about it!). The next activity is about learning to count syllables. Many text-books offer haiku as a model, but although there is a British version that insists that the pattern is 5, 7, 5 syllables, there is a problem with emulating the original, as the Japanese concept of a syllable is very, very different from our own.

## ACTIVITY

Write a poem in which each line has seven syllables. It really doesn't matter what the subject is, or how good it is. However, suggesting an odd (as against even) number of syllables is not accidental. Writing to an even number of syllables may well tend to make you give the poem an alternate beat (in which case, once again, why write in syllabics?).

The only rule is not to break a word with a hyphen (e.g. foll-/ow) as you go over a line. It's up to you but three to five five-line stanzas would be sufficient. And never do this competitively with a musician, by the way. They can count! You can choose any subject, but I suggest that you make it conversational, and insist that you use contemporary language.

## DISCUSSION

I wonder how you fared. My guess is that you spent a great deal of time counting and cursing, and perhaps worrying about words like 'hour' which seem to have one syllable one moment, and two the next. When in doubt, stop worrying. You will also perhaps have written a little too monosyllabically (easier to count), if this is the first time you've tried it; and you may have resorted to filler words like 'just' to solve a problem. You may also have stopped every line, or most of them, with a full stop or other punctuation. All of this is fine. Here's my effort. I chose to write about an auction.

> The gavel crunches and the
> lot is flogged. Someone has lost
> an heirloom to a stranger,
> and the stranger, dizzily,
> is taking their past away.

> The worthless expert recoils
> to find her estimate has
> been wildly overshot. She
> hardens her grin of surprise
> until she looks like porcelain.

There is little to commend this other than that it has seven syllables in each line, and that there is some repetition and assonance in the first half. I have counted correctly: that's all. But now let me let you into a simple secret. The Dylan Thomas poem 'Over Sir John's Hill' breaks a number of rules, and slightly varies the syllable count. It even splits the word 'jackdaws' across a line. On the other hand, Thomas not only decided to work with a complex rhyme-scheme as well (*aabccbdeaedd*), but to make the *d* rhyme, in each stanza, fall on the penultimate syllable in the line: a very demanding task! It's a familiar saw: break the rules when you know them.

I'll finish this section by issuing you with a challenge. Go back to your poem and rewrite it; only, this time, make sure each line has the same number of beats or stresses (probably three in a seven-syllable line). The likelihood is that you have already done this without thinking. And try to cross from one line to another, as in

> Someone has lost
> an heirloom to a stranger, ...

# Writing in a poetic voice

Starting to write a poem can seem a daunting prospect. To begin with, however, you are only going to try some limbering-up exercises, and what you write may well seem rough and ready. This is an important part of the process, however. Nearly all the poems you have read will have started from a few jotted notes of observation, or a phrase the writer has overheard, or a very vague idea. It is important, though, that you focus on using contemporary language, and stay away from the many archaisms that spring to mind when thinking about poems you may have come across, and enjoyed, and even remembered well enough to quote. Here are some examples of the kind of word I'm thinking of:

> wondrous, drear, bedecked, 'tis, mead, yonder, pent, mourn, naught, musing, adorn, vale, wilt, shalt, thou, thee, citadel, aplenty, woe, wrought, forlorn, saith, brow, avail, wherefore, o'er.

It is difficult to be prescriptive – in the right context, 'mourn' might be appropriate, for instance – but avoid words that you would not hear in everyday conversation, for which there are good alternatives. The words cited above are the kind frequently used in Victorian hymns, or memories of Romantic poets studied in school-days. This doesn't mean you can't raid the dictionary: there are some words just itching to be rescued and reused. The words to edit out of your poetic vocabulary are those that sound as if they've been borrowed from poems written a hundred or more years ago. Notice that this is *exactly* the same advice as I gave about historical fiction in Chapter 7: you are a contemporary writer. Use contemporary language. John Whitworth nails this most neatly: 'But why write like Keats? Keats wrote supremely well. Why not write like yourself?' (Whitworth, 2006 [2001], p. 9)

Equally, it's a good idea to stick to natural word order. You wouldn't hear anyone say 'To the shops shall I go'. They'd more probably say 'I'm off to the shops'. When you invert the natural order of words, especially if you do it to make a rhyme fit, the result generally sounds clunky. Two other suggestions at this stage are to avoid abstract nouns (e.g. obedience, love, hate, desire, anxiety, and so on), choosing instead to show the mood or quality you are describing, and to stay away from clusters of multisyllabic words. The power of a contemporary poetic voice comes from its skill with sound, structure, image and idea – and also from its being creative but unforced, especially in its rhythm.

## ACTIVITY

Create a list of twenty words with a long *a* sound in them in which the weight of the pronunciation falls on that syllable. A long *a* sound is as in 'g*a*le', '*a*geing', 'def*a*me', 'w*ei*ght', 'betr*a*yal', 'pass*é*', 'f*ai*ling', 'f*a*ded', 'constr*ai*nt', 'cr*a*dle'. Notice that the spelling of the long *a* sound can vary. In the examples given here, it is on the *a* sound that the beat falls; other words may also have a long *a* sound (depending on your accent of course), for example 'amoral', 'régime' and 'portrait', but in these words the weight falls on -*mor*, -*gime* and *port*-respectively. Choose eight of these twenty words.

Now look at the photograph below and write eight single-sentence statements from the point of view of either of the people in it, or the photographer, who captioned the poem 'Three Beauties'. Each statement must contain one or more of the words you have selected. The statements do not have to start with the word 'I'.

*'Three Beauties'*

134

## DISCUSSION

You may have found that your list of statements was very peculiar, that they varied in length or that you found yourself making unconscious connections between them. For this activity, it doesn't matter. However, notice that I have been quite restrictive in what you can do. Not only have I given you a specific photograph from which to work, but I have also specified a vowel sound that has to appear in each of the lines. This is because, when you are practising writing, it is usually best to operate under some constraint. If I offered you the whole of the English language and an infinite choice of images, the sheer range of possibilities would probably overwhelm you. Restricting yourself in some way creates the tension that is essential to composing words. (You have the additional constraint of the photograph, too – a constraint often used in creative writing workshops to relax writers who are worrying about choice of subject.) Here is a list of statements I've invented:

> My aim is to act on the stage.
> My favourite is hard to choose.
> I'm afraid that I've parked at an angle.
> I'm staking my claim as a beauty.
> I'd rather be here than in the shade.
> I am not playing and wait here with folded arms.
> The trail wanders off into the distance.
> I have no intention of waving.

For obvious reasons, this list contains a great deal of echo and some internal rhyme ('aim'/'claim'/, and 'afraid'/'shade'). It may be that your own list has some hidden rhymes, as well – and it will certainly have some echo, because I designed the exercise so that it would.

As it stands, its potential as a poem is spoiled by the repeated end-stopping (the eight full stops at the end of each line). To draft a coherent whole, it will almost invariably be better for the sentences to move across the lines.

---

Making notes is only the first stage, and, in this case, the notes have been constrained by showing you how sound patterns might emerge. Poems about photographs or paintings are a good way of trying out voices, because they focus your imagination: the detail of what your image looks like is predetermined, although of course the choice of language you might use to describe it is open. A poem about the photograph here might go in any one of dozens of different directions. These directions can't be pre-planned - a poem, like a story, will find its own way. Nonetheless, I've tried two drafts of a poem based partly on the painting and partly on my eight statements. The first one is shown below. It's handwritten, although it really is a matter of preference how you write. Handwritten drafts have the advantage of allowing you to see the changes you have made more easily.

You can see that I have made a sort of false start, and also that I have attempted to control the movement by using three-line stanzas. This was not a planned decision; a writer tends to light on a structure while writing. I have now started to move across the line-endings to give the poem more fluidity. I have also kept the following words from my original eight lines: 'shade', 'trail', 'wave', 'wait'. I'm certainly not going to be able to use only the long *a* sound in the poem: that would make it too repetitive. I have added other echoes instead. In places I have tried some choices.

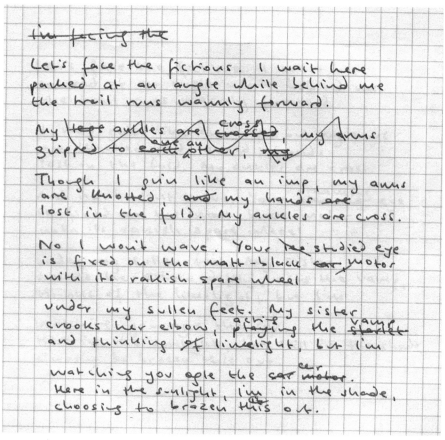

*First draft of a poem based on 'Three Beauties'*

By the second draft I have made several changes.

> Let's face the fictions. I wait here
> parked at an angle while behind me
> the trail runs warmly forward.
>
> I may grin like an imp, but my arms
> are knotted and locked, hands
> lost in the fold. My ankles are cross.
>
> And no I won't wave. Your dreaming eye
> is fixed on the matt-black motor
> with its rakish spare wheel
>
> under my sullen feet. My sister
> crooks her elbow deftly, acts the vamp,
> thinks of the limelight, but I'm
>
> watching you ogle the car.
> Here in the sunlight, I'm still in the shade,
> choosing to brazen this out.

*Second draft of a poem based on 'Three Beauties'*

At this stage (for this is far from a finished poem), I have focused on the girl on the roof, although I began with the car, and changed the focus from the car to the girl on the roof when it occurred to me that both were 'parked at an angle' (another phrase kept from the original exercise), even though this may well be the photographer's fault. It helped me to have one speaker (notice how this is very similar to the process of restricting the narrative voice described in Chapter 7). The process of writing is very much about finding a subject. The original exercise was simply to help me think, and to see if I could find some harmonies ('brazen' and 'rakish' were almost certainly the by-product of the experiment with the long *a* sound). The original writing about the photograph is an exercise, not necessarily an outcome in itself: the poem could have gone, and may yet go, anywhere.

Using black-and-white photographs can be helpful, as colour can be distracting: monochrome forces you to use your imagination. I have an advantage and a disadvantage over you with this photograph. I know who took it (my mother's elder brother, the owner of the car), that it was taken in 1929 in Norfolk, and that the girl to the left, my mother's elder sister, did wish to be an actress (and became one). And it's my mother, aged six, on the roof of the car. So the *context* of my writing is different than if you were to look at the same photograph and to write a poem based on it. It's also distracting for me, because I know a bit too much, and I may be making the poem too private by using that knowledge. Incidentally, writing about photographs does often lead a writer to consider the actual relationship between the photographer and the subject. That's certainly the case with the next activity.

---

## ACTIVITY

The photograph opposite is an iconic image from an edition of *Vogue* magazine from 1930, taken by George Hoyningen-Huene. Try using this image as the basis for some notes towards creating a poem, beginning by creating a series of statements in which there is a vowel-echo. You might like to try drafting the opening of a poem based on this photograph.

## DISCUSSION

One of the decisions you will have had to make is who your speaker will be. One of the divers? The photographer? Yourself? Your representative? And what aspects of the photograph will you have focused upon? The stillness? The way their heads are turned away? The line of the horizon? The monochrome?

The poet Maura Dooley used this photograph as the basis for her poem 'Bathers, 1930'.

*George Hoyningen-Huene, 'Divers'. From* Vogue, *5 July 1930. Photo: © Condé Nast Archives/Corbis*

**Bathers, 1930**

*(from a photograph by George Hoyningen-Huene)*

Staring so intently out to sea
they do not hear the stealthy camera
click like a key in a lock.

His hair is thick, sticky with salt.
Her hair is shingled. Their skins take a dip
in June sunlight. The air, the mood is blue.

The rest is out of focus; an ocean corrugates
and concertinas, the wind is a held breath,
the horizon too distant to believe in.
Their faces turned from us, they balance
on the edge of a narrow jetty. We look at them,
in black and white, from a long way off.

                    (Dooley, 1990, p. 61)

What Dooley has done in this poem is to focus on the difficulty of interpreting the image, and (not unlike Draycott in 'Golf') on the way the couple is perpetually 'distant' or 'a long way off'. Notice also how the voice of this poem, which is reflective and reserved, is created for us by a quiet pattern of echoes, by the way the vowels recur and resonate, and even by the stealthy use of internal rhyme ('click'/'thick'/'sticky'). Dooley also shows us a very good example of where and why to break a line:

> they balance
> on the edge of a narrow jetty.

The line-break gives us a fractional moment in which to experience that sense of teetering on an edge. Another quality to take away from this poem is its careful use of contemporary word order and vocabulary. (It is worth noting at this point that Dooley used the photograph 'Divers' as the inspiration for her poem, but it was not printed with the poem. It is rare that pictures and poems are published side by side – the picture may be the starting point, but the poem has to stand by itself.)

# The tone of poetic voice

Because I specified the use of long vowel sounds at the start of the activity before last, I have, at least at this stage, dictated the tone of the drafts of the accompanying poem, which is one of slightly moody introspection. The long vowel sounds have slowed the pace. The pattern of sound, and the accompanying rhythm could dictate an entirely different mood. To give you an example, if the voice was to be hesitant, I would expect there to be far more breaks, and more changes in pace.

> I might perhaps
>     suspect that
>   a hesitant poem would
>   use breaks
> more frequently, that it would
>    vary the rhythms, or possess
>     a slightly unsettling
>   and tentative pattern.

## ACTIVITY

See if you can create examples of short poetic extracts which aim to have one of the following kinds of voice:

| | | | | |
|---|---|---|---|---|
| angry | carefree | thoughtful | jaunty | mournful |
| precise | excitable | meditative | intimate | scatterbrained |

the adjectives suggested are not mutually exclusive – feel free to combine two, if you wish, or to try others. Think about what kinds of rhythm you might use. Think also about the importance of echo.

## DISCUSSION

In the process of experiment, you probably considered most if not all of the following ways in which you might achieve the chosen voice, in addition to your use of echo and rhythm:

1. whether the voice was your own, or the voice of someone else

2. what kind of vocabulary you should use

3. how many breaks or pauses you should introduce

4. how you could imply the mood, rather than explain it

5. whether to use end-rhyme, internal rhyme, half-rhyme

6. the potential length of the piece

7. how you might lay the piece out on the page.

---

We will now consider some examples of how you might create voices that are (although I could use other adjectives) thoughtful, jaunty and angry – that have distinctive identities. After each type of voice is discussed, there is a brief activity that gives you the opportunity to try drafting a few lines in that voice. There is a discussion of all three activities at the end of the last one.

*'Thoughtful'*
Achieving a thoughtful, perhaps quizzical tone of voice in a poem may mean writing in a looser, more clearly conversational tone, one in which there is a degree of intimacy set up with the reader. If you've ever read any poems by Billy Collins – and I recommend 'Forgetfulness' in *Sailing Alone Around the Room* (2001) – you'll see that his voice is genial, almost casual in tone: practically a drawl. Collins himself, discussing the teaching of poetry, has remarked that understanding tone is the key to meaning:

> I think teaching [students] how to read a poem involves conveying what tone is. And when you convey the tone, you're really conveying the spirit of the poem. That's more important than whatever passes for meaning. If they get the tone of voice, that's almost enough to direct them through the poem and replace or at least quiet the anxiety about what the poem means.
>
> (Collins, n.d.)

A conversational tone is used by Michael Laskey in his poem 'Lesson'.

**Lesson**

Five minutes, no more, our stroll
from the restaurant through the quiet
Sunday afternoon streets,
headed for our books, the next chapter
a bench in the park or stretched out
under trees on the grass. We were crossing
the Paseo del Prado when you noticed
my backpack gaping, unzipped,

the wallet gone, no longer mine.
Apparently it's always happening
with backpacks, but after the shock
and the hassle, it's the deftness
I'm left with, how I didn't feel a thing,
how you need to keep practising.

(Laskey, 2008, p. 100)

The thoughtful voice here is achieved by a great deal of understatement, and also by the intimacy of the address from 'I' to 'you', as if it were a private conversation. The movement across the lines is unobtrusive, and the rhythm mirrors the steady pace of the events. The words which denote pace – 'stroll', 'headed', 'crossing' – are not sudden at all, and the key word 'noticed' is undemonstrative. One of the key words defining the voice is 'Apparently'. There is a brief – very brief – moment recording the 'shock/and the hassle', in which the word 'shock', with its harder final consonant, appears at the end of the line. But the poem moves quietly forward, using the subtle echo of 'left' and 'deft' to turn the 'lesson' of the event into one quite opposite to what we might have imagined of the speaker. The lesson is not about learning to remember to zip your backpack, but an understanding of the practice that a thief must have to undertake – the lesson the thief must learn. The quiet near-rhymes of 'thing'/'practising' at the ends of the final two lines ensure that the voice remains quiet, meditative, discursive. If the last two lines had finished with the beat falling on a full rhyme (say, 'thing'/'sting'), the ending would have been too emphatic for the voice in the poem's purpose.

---

## ACTIVITY

Write four or five lines of a draft poem in which, as in 'Lesson', you are describing something surprising, but doing so in a calm and thoughtful way. You are free to choose any subject, but here is one to try: a car passing you at great speed, forcing you to jump out of the way.

---

### 'Jaunty'

Jauntiness implies an up-tempo beat, and tempo is crucial to the identity of a poetic voice. The beat is plainly going to be more pronounced in an up-tempo poem. A jaunty voice is an enthusiastic voice, one that takes ostentatious pleasure in what it says. This is a voice, therefore, that might well be helped by a rhyme-scheme. Here is a brief poem about examinations:

The question is quick;
The question is dreary.
I'm already sick
Of narrative theory.

I've written my name
But my answer's glib:
Marker, take aim
With your moist red nib.

This poem hops along with miserable glee. The repetitions now extend to rhyming, and the phrasal repetitions are more ostentatious. The slangy vocabulary breezes along. Notice here that the rhymes give the emphasis: there is only a little echo on the vowel sounds, and only a little alliteration ('marker'/'moist') to energise the sound of the poem. (Alliteration is in my view a very over-rated means of giving a poem a sense of wholeness.) The rhyme scheme – *abab* – helps us understand that this is a comic voice. By contrast, here is an extract from 'The Examiners' by John Whitworth (the first and last stanzas of five).

Where the house is cold and empty and the garden's overgrown,
They are there.
Where the letters lie unopened by a disconnected phone,
They are there.
Where your footsteps echo strangely on each moonlit cobblestone,
Where a shadow streams behind you but the shadow's not your own,
You may think the world's your oyster but it's bone, bone, bone:
They are there, they are there, they are there.
[...]

They are there, they are there like a whisper on the air,
They are there.
They are slippery and soapy with our hope and our despair,
They are there.
So it's idle if we bridle or pretend we never care,
If the questions are superfluous and the marking isn't fair,
For we know they're going to get us, we just don't know when or where,
They are there, they are there, they are there.

(Whitworth, 2007, p. 21)

This is a sinister voice, but at the same time it is comically sinister, because of the sheer extent of the rhyme and echo. The first stanza offers us two rhymes – and uses four end-rhymes on the syllable *-one*, which it reinforces with the repetition of 'bone'; and there are four, arguably five, further long *o* sounds (because it is very tempting here to give a long *o* to disconnected). What you will have to decide is whether you think the voice is sufficiently sinister to create a momentary frisson or fright. In the last stanza, it uses the refrain *-ere* (pronounced 'air') rhyme no fewer than thirteen times. I would argue that it is the voice of a music-hall or stage villain, partly because of the ostentation of internal rhymes like 'idle' and 'bridle', and partly because of the contrasting rhythms – the tiptoeing, pattering rhythm of the long lines and the short, slightly melodramatic refrains. But the voice is certainly more disturbing than the voice in the first poem.

---

## ACTIVITY

Write two lines to match the line below, making sure that the beat is lively and that the same rhyme is used at the end of each line. Start each line with the given phrase 'Open up'. You can write on any subject, but if you'd rather, use anything that is suggested by the title 'Under Arrest'.

Open up the window with a hammer or a chisel …

---

*'Angry'*

Outright, splenetic rage is exceptionally hard to manage in a poem. Controlled anger, which will carry more force, and run less risk of being comic, needs to be emphatic, direct. The poem 'A Cold Coming' by Tony Harrison, inspired by the image of the charred head of an Iraqi soldier in a blown-up vehicle, was published in *The Guardian* during the First Gulf War in 1991 (it was reprinted in 2003). It opens with the following lines:

> I saw the charred Iraqi lean towards me from bomb-blasted screen,
> his windscreen wiper like a pen ready to write down thoughts for men,
> his windscreen wiper like a quill he's reaching for to make his will.
> I saw the charred Iraqi lean like someone made of Plasticine
> as though he'd stopped to ask the way and this is what I heard him say:
> 'Don't be afraid I've picked on you for this exclusive interview.
> Isn't it your sort of poet's task to find words for this frightening mask?
> If that gadget that you've got records words from such scorched vocal cords,
> press RECORD before some dog devours me mid-monologue.'
> (Harrison, 2003 [1991], p. 12)

In this poem, which possesses considerable authority, the bitterness is controlled by the rhymes (which appear halfway through the lines), and by the general firmness of the rhythm. Harrison makes the most of his invective by repeating phrases and also sounds (in 'charred Iraqi', and 'windscreen wiper', for instance), and by not only using a colloquial, naturally ordered language, but also by including direct and monosyllabic phrases ('and this is what I heard him say'). It is intense and fierce; but it does not shout. The authority of this poem was extended not only by its publication in a national newspaper, but also by the publication next to it of the grim photograph that inspired it.

Harrison's savage poem is both personal and political. There are other kinds of anger, as in this extract from 'Ill-Wishing Him' by Dorothy Nimmo, in which a wife sardonically recounts what she wishes had happened to a husband who has left her.

> I wish he'd had to rent a room
> in Peterborough, to take his washing
> to the launderette, watch his shirts turn pink.
> I wish he'd lived on pork-pie and pizza
> and it had made him sick.
> I wish he'd gone senile and forgotten
> who he was and what he'd done
> and every day I could remind him. I wish
> he'd died and left my name
> as next of kin. They'd ring me
> and I'd say, *Never heard of him*.
> (Nimmo, 2000, p. 12)

Once again, notice the importance of the repetitions at both the phrasal ('I wish') and syllable level ('wash'/'watch', 'it'/'sick', 'kin'/'ring'), and the accessibility of the language. The poetic voice is made stronger by the incremental nature of the curses. It makes the voice vicious and comic at the same time.

---

## ACTIVITY

Find a story or an article in a daily newspaper in which one person is complaining about the actions of another (this should not be hard!). Write the draft opening of a poem – four or five lines – in which you use the voice of the complainant to express your anger with the other person. Think of a repetitive phrase that will bind the opening together.

## DISCUSSION

In each of three activities in this section, you have been experimenting with creating a first draft. In each case, you have been asked to make a conscious effort to use rhythm, repetition or beat to establish the tone. In other words, you have been asked to make a conscious effort to create a voice, much more conscious than if you were simply talking to someone or writing a casual email or letter, and more conscious too than if you were writing prose. Poetry is a more conscious art-form, as I suggested above: the trick is not to make it self-conscious. That is not to say that the use of words is never ostentatious. Poetic voices are by nature ostentatious – the degree of ostentation depends on the nature of the voice you are creating.

# Giving poetry power

Poems are often used at solemn or serious occasions because poetic form can possess authority – Harrison's poem was a very public poem, and the context of its publication enhanced that. The kind of authority I have in mind is not the poetry which is, as it were, licensed by the state. The long history of the laureateship in Great Britain has never been known to produce poems of any special character (see the box on laureateship for a brief note on this). For instance, in 1852 Tennyson wrote an ode on the Duke of Wellington, published on the morning of his funeral, that begins

> Bury the Great Duke
>    With an empire's lamentation;
> Let us bury the Great Duke
>    To the noise of the mourning of a mighty nation;
> Mourning when their leaders fall,
> Warriors carry the warrior's pall,
> And sorrow darkens hamlet and hall.
>            (Tennyson, 1963 [1852], p. 156)

The ode continues for a further 274 lines. It was received with 'all but Universal deprecation' (Hibbert, 1998, p. 402). Almost all laureate poems have received a less than enthusiastic response, although the incumbent, Carol Ann Duffy, has been praised for her work.

## Laureateship

The post of poet laureate is a royal appointment, with a history going back at least to the seventeenth century and probably much further, to the thirteenth century, or even earlier. The duties of the laureate were, historically, to write public poetry in honour or celebration of national events. From 1670 to 1998, the post was for life. In 1998, tenure was limited to ten years, and the second to hold the post under this rule is Carol Ann Duffy, the first woman to be given the post. She has promised to be more wide-ranging in her choice of subject. There have been many poets who have turned the post down, including Thomas Gray (1716–71), who said he would rather be 'pin-maker to the palace'. William Wordsworth (1770–1850) took the post on the strict condition that he would not be obliged to write any laureate verse (he never did).

In poetry, the power of a voice will often come not from its public but its private quality. It will come from its intimacy, and, if it is to carry any real authority, from a mixture of complexity and emotional honesty. An authoritative voice is one that requires you to listen, not merely to hear.

The authority of a writer stems, too, not from the depiction of character but from the clarity and emotional force of the writer's voice, a voice that should be neither strident nor didactic nor dogmatic. What the reader responds to is the control and force of the language, the manipulation of voice so that it conducts and encourages debate. In contemporary poetry, this might well be called a degree of truth, a presentation of language that is at once intimate and colloquial while also formally compelling. To put it more simply, the poetry has to be distinctive and personal.

## ACTIVITY

Read the poem 'Honour Killing' by Imtiaz Dharker. Can you suggest ways in which the voice she uses might be said to carry authority? Think about the way the lines and stanzas are arranged, the way that the poem develops, the language that it uses.

### Honour Killing

At last I'm taking off this coat,
  this black coat of a country
  that I swore for years was mine,
  that I wore more out of habit

than design.
Born wearing it,
I believed I had no choice.

I'm taking off this veil,
   this black veil of a faith
   that made me faithless
   to myself,
   that tied my mouth,
   gave my god a devil's face,
   and muffled my own voice.

I'm taking off these silks,
   these lacy things
   that feed dictator dreams,
   the mangalsutra and the rings
   rattling in a tin cup of needs
   that beggared me.

I'm taking off this skin,
   and then the face, the flesh,
   the womb.

Let's see
   what I am in here
   when I squeeze past
   the easy cage of bone.

Let's see
   what I am out here,
   making, crafting,
   plotting
   at my new geography.

## DISCUSSION

In my view, what gives this poem authority is that it fuses the public and the personal. We hear the speaker, but we also understand what the writer's attitude is to her, a mixture of empathy and pain for her predicament. Indeed, perhaps we can't be sure who is 'taking off' coat, veil, silks – it might be Dharker herself, it might be the speaker she has created. Many tactics are used here. The tone is cool and collected, at odds with the subject, which seems to be about a woman discarding her nationality, her faith, her marriage and then, more surreally, her physical self. The tension between the tone and the subject is what forces the reader to concentrate: this too gives the poem authority. The vocabulary is not complex. Perhaps some of us would need to be told what a mangalsutra is (a golden ornament tied by thread around the neck of a bride, by the bridegroom, in a Hindu wedding ceremony), but the poem is highly accessible. This too gives it authority. So too does the repetition, the incantation of the poem, the repeated lines 'I'm taking off ...', which lead to the repeated 'Let's see ...'. The repetition is also present at a more subliminal level – the repetition of 'black', the repetition of 'that' and 'what', the repetition of the sounds in 'swore'/'wore', 'feed'/'needs', 'squeeze'/'easy', the concluding short o sound in 'plotting' and 'geography'. These repetitions feed the intensity of the poem, which arrives, through the ambiguity of 'plotting', at a moment of decision. The poem possesses what I referred to above: emotional honesty. And, troublingly perhaps, we are kept in check throughout the poem by that title: 'Honour Killing'. We have to decide what is happening. We might wonder what sparked the poem (which was the murder, by her own family, of a woman who wanted a divorce). However, notice that Dharker, who is a Scots Muslim by birth, but whose partner is Hindu, does not direct us in a journalistic way. The voice does not belong to a specific woman, but to a representative of all women. No mention of specific faith is made. The poem has authority because it does not offer an argument but an exploration, and because it develops in a quizzical and unpredictable way, the stanzas shortening as it comes to its point.

---

Dharker's poem offers you many examples of how to invest writing with authority: repetition; echo; tension; simplicity of language, but a degree of complexity; development; a personal subject with broader political implications. Perhaps it also carries authority because it possesses only partially suppressed rage. And, of course, its authority comes from the fact that it is attacking another authority. The reference for a DVD version of her speaking the poem is given in the bibliography at the end of the book, in which her eloquence is magnified by her stillness, and by the fact that she is not reading but speaking the poem. With poetry, we often move into the same territory inhabited by theatre – of live art. In the next activity you can use some of these techniques to produce some writing of your own.

---

## ACTIVITY

Choose a subject about which you feel passionate. It might come from something you have read about, or even something that has happened to you – but beware the side-effect of writing something very personal. Writing directly about your own life may prevent you from distancing yourself from the subject sufficiently. When you have chosen your subject, set down what you feel about it in the form of a series of statements, beginning, if you like, 'This is …' or 'Whenever I …'. Don't worry about making your statements rhyme. What you should have at the end of the activity is the framework for a poem, not necessarily a poem itself.

## DISCUSSION

What you have written is the draft of what is known as a 'list poem', and sometimes as a 'litany poem', in which successive statements repeat, amend, expand and amplify earlier ones. This kind of repetition is a characteristic of many religious chants or songs.

List poems can also be entertaining. The poem 'Spider' by Geoff Hattersley, an elegy to a spider he has just squashed, is a parody of the same technique – making fun by exploring the spider's non-human existence, while at the same time investigating the very human attributes it lacks, all the while repeating 'It never…' at the opening of each line.

> The spider was completely unprepared
> for assault from above by an ash-tray,
> it never had a friend it could count on.
> It never knew its blood-group.
> It never saw itself changing, or any need to.
> It never said: 'No more excuses.'
> It never felt tempted by drugs.
> It never knew the itch to the nearest bar.
> Its earning power was never an issue.
> It was never hurt by a few home-truths.
> It never did anything for anyone.
> It never knew the myth of Wyatt Earp.
> It never hoped for more than was likely.
> It never had Watchtower thrust at it.
> It never saw a rainbow, or a bunch of flowers
>                     dropped into an open grave.
> It never wrote an essay on the works of Alexander Pope.
> It never filled in an application form.
> It never married for love or money.
> It never had a honeymoon in a hotel.
> It never knew who was Prime Minister.
> It never knew if it was lucky or not.
> It never shopped for clothes.
> It never smiled.
> It never felt like a paperclip

in a jar in a cupboard in a shed.
It never carried a briefcase.
It never missed the last train.
It never slept off a hangover.
It never thought it was Marlon Brando.
(Hattersley, 1994, p. 47)

What gives authority to Hattersley's enjoyably daft poem (which continues for a further ninety lines) is the resonance of repetition. If you work on your own piece, seeing if you can put the statements in the most interesting order, you will have a poem on your hands, and one that has the authority not just of the written word but of incantation – by implication, the spoken voice.

---

## Developing a subject for a poem and experimenting with language

In this chapter so far, you have looked at the way that poetry, as a verbal art, is highly conscious of its use of language, and is more conscious of itself as possessing an invented voice, one that is shaped, rhythmic, musical. But understanding the technique might reasonably be said to be secondary to having a subject about which to write a poetic text. As I have suggested with the 'Three Beauties' activity, a poem can start in one place, and take the writer into a different, surprising direction. There are many techniques for activating the creative impulse, and space precludes listing them all here. As a coda to this chapter though, let me discuss two particular ways of doing this.

One way is to begin with a constraint - it might be a specific form, it might be using a picture as a starting point. You might be surprised to learn that Jane Draycott's poem 'Golf' which you looked at earlier in the chapter is one of a sequence of twenty-six poems based on the words used by the NATO Phonetic Alphabet, which uses code-words for letters: *alpha, bravo, charlie, delta, echo, foxtrot, golf*, etc. What Draycott has done is to force her imagination to work by challenging it: the title is dictated by the sequence of the code-words. She has forced herself to draw observations and images out of the game of golf, in which she has no inherent interest. The constraint of the title is what forces her to think, to create.

While it is true that there are many famous long narrative poems in the English language, most poems are comparatively short. This is because they find their voice by focusing on an incident (the dropping of an ashtray on a spider, the theft of a wallet from a backpack, seeing a photo of two bathers). Poems, as texts, are very much about capturing and interpreting a moment, and seeing what potential for exploration there is within that moment. It may help to think of a poem as a photograph, rather than as a film narrative. In poetry, creative writing is often sparked by a single image, one that is given added resonance by the kinds of tricks of sound and rhythm explored above.

The poetic voices to which you have been introduced so far have been reasonably and recognisably conversational, but, as the prose extracts at the start of this chapter show, voices can be more complex, more subtle, more experimental with language. As long as you think the reader will understand what you write, there is no reason why the language should not become more elliptical, more concentrated. And actually, you may find it good fun to experiment with sound patterns so that, at least to start with, you are the only one in complete control of the sound. Many poets write about wind or sea, but they tend to use wind or sea as setting. You could write about pure and elemental natural forces, and that might lead you to experiment quite interestingly with sound effects. There is an element of the purely sonic in poetry. A wonderful example of this is a poem by the Australian poet Les Murray, called 'Shoal', which appears in his collection *Translations from the Natural World* (1993). It inhabits the collective mind of a shoal of fish. A composer, Damian Ricketson, set it to music for six unaccompanied voices in 2003, and turned it into pure and startling sound. There is a thin line between poetry and music, and I will leave you with the thought that it is occasionally worth crossing.

In summary, then, we have looked in this chapter at the way in which writing 'poetic language', and writing poetry itself, means harnessing a variety of techniques. We have also explored how these poetic techniques mean introducing subtle new resonance into writing, resonance that uses language in a consciously inventive way, one that moves closer along a continuum towards music. Finally, we have looked at creative writing in a way that is intended to show that writing and reading are inseparable: testing yourself as a creative writer means that you will be a more informed reader, just as being a more informed reader will make you a more successful creative writer.

# Afterword: how we shape language to express ourselves

Over the course of this book we've looked at the many multifaceted elements of language, and how these are used in acts of creativity and expression. A key theme has been the way that meaning is conveyed not simply by the content of utterances (i.e. by the way the words refer to things and ideas in the world), but also by their form, structure and patterning. The sounds of words, the manner in which they are combined, the expectations they produce in a reader or audience – all these things contribute to the overall meaning of the utterance. We've seen how this happens in a variety of textual and communicative genres, ranging from newspaper reports and job interviews to short stories, popular songs and poetry. We've also looked at how language operates as a marker of identity and how the type of language one speaks (in terms of one's accent, dialect and choice of register) has a strong relationship to the communities one belongs to.

In parallel to this we've looked at the strategies that creative writers employ to exploit the expressive potential of language, and at how they play with language and edit and reshape it to create images and characters, voices and stories. In the final chapter we looked at instances of composition where the manipulation of language is able to achieve an almost musical effect, and where the referential content of the words (what they 'mean' in terms of objects and concepts) is secondary to the patterns of sound achieved by their artful arrangement. If language were reduced to a scheme that did nothing more than refer to objects out there in the real world – as was parodied in the excerpt from *Gulliver's Travels* that we looked at in the Introduction – none of this would be possible. Language would be a mundane and limited tool, instead of the rich and adaptive resource it actually is.

Another key issue that has emerged through the course of the book is that this type of meaning can also have a powerful social and political effect. People are constantly being evaluated in terms of their use of language, whether it be the type of accent they have or the way they answer a question in a job interview. Newspapers and other forms of media frame a view of the world through the way they organise the language of their reports. And creative writers can draw on forms of indirect meaning to express the complexities of human experience, as, for example, in Imtiaz Dharker's poem 'Honour Killing' (Chapter 9). Often the subtleties of this type of meaning are not immediately apparent. They are hidden in the structure of a piece of discourse, in the subtext of a narrative, or in the interplay of form and content in a poem. By looking at how the process of expression happens, though, and at the nature of the resources that we use to communicate, we can gain a better idea of what's involved in the creation of texts, and of how they operate as powerful means of both personal and social expression.

The book has focused on the language from which texts are assembled, and the writing processes by which they are composed. Our aim has been to explore the way that meaning is made by the artful manipulation of language. For if, as Ben Jonson suggested, language is 'the only benefit man hath to expresse his excellencie of mind above other creatures' (1947 [1641], pp. 620-1), it is in the composition of culturally resonant texts that this benefit is most fully realised – and the purpose of this book has been to take a closer look at what is involved in this composition, and at how we shape language to express ourselves.

# Glossary

**academic register**   see **register**.

**accent**   the features of pronunciation that indicate a person's regional or social background. The term refers specifically to pronunciation, while the term **dialect** is used to refer to differences in **grammar** and vocabulary.

**adjacency pair**   a sequence of turns in a conversation in which the first utterance provokes a particular category of response. For example, a question is typically followed by an answer, while an invitation is typically followed by an acceptance or rejection.

**alliteration**   the repetition of a consonantal sound, especially at the beginning of words.

**assonance**   the repetition of a vowel sound.

**audience**   can conventionally mean those who watch a play (although it actually means 'listening'!) or film. However, it is often used as a general term for anyone for whom a creative writer composes. For example, we can talk of a novelist's audience.

**back-story**   the events that have taken place before the action of a story starts, and that we learn about during the story.

**conversation analysis**   the study of how conversational interaction is structured.

**dialect**   a language variety in which aspects of the vocabulary and **grammar** indicate a person's regional or social background. It is contrasted with **accent**, which refers specifically to differences in pronunciation.

**dialogue**   conversation between two or more characters.

**discourse**   a term that has a variety of slightly different meanings related to Language Studies. In this module, it's being used to refer to sequences of connected speech or writing, usually made up of more than one sentence.

**discourse community**   a social group who have common interests and who use a particular **register** of language (composed of specialist vocabulary and particular **genres**) when they are pursuing those interests.

**drafting**   the process of writing and rewriting through which a writer goes in the process of composing.

**foregrounding**   producing a (literary) effect in a text by drawing attention to the use of language itself, often by purposely deviating from the way that everyday speech is constructed

**free indirect speech**   a technique for allowing the reader to see into a character's mind, even when a piece of fiction is written in the third person.

**genre**   in the context of Language Studies, the term 'genre' refers to the different types of communicative act, which are distinguished from each other by the form they take and the purpose they have. For example, a letter is a particular type of genre, as is a job interview or a political speech. In each case, there are conventional patterns in the way the communicative act is organised, and the purpose it is designed to fulfil. In the context of Literature and Creative Writing, 'genre' has two related meanings. It can mean a particular type of writing, for instance, poetry, fiction, life writing, drama. It can also mean a subset of these, so that in fiction it could mean a novel or short story, or particular types of these, such as romance, crime, horror, fantasy, etc. (The term 'genre fiction' is often used to describe what are properly sub-genres.) Poetry might be lyric poetry or comic poetry or narrative poetry, and so on. Drama might be divided by medium, so that the word 'genre' could be used of screenplay, stage play, radio play.

**genre fiction**   see **genre**.

**grammar**   the way a language is structured. It is often used to refer in particular to the way in which words and their component parts (e.g. word endings that denote tense) combine to form sentences.

**International Phonetic Alphabet (IPA)**   a specialised system for transcribing the speech sounds of language.

**language variation**   the way in which the forms and structures of a language vary according to its users and to the circumstances in which it is used.

**life writing**   an umbrella term that covers autobiography and biography. It often uses techniques associated with fiction, and there are particular strands of it that are individually identified, such as travel writing. Its central focus is, as the term implies, the story of all or part of a life.

**Linguistics**    the term used for the general study of language.

**metaphor**    a figure of speech in which two different things are implicitly compared, as in 'the grass bristled'; see also **simile**.

**mode**    the actual means by which a message is communicated. For example, the mode could be speech (the use of the voice), or writing, or, in the case of sign language, gestures. Different modes of communication have different possibilities and limitations, which result in different forms of language being associated with them.

**monologue**    a speech delivered by one individual, on their own, to an audience or reader.

**narrator**    the person who relays a story to readers. The narrator may be an uninvolved voice created by the writer, who 'knows' all or most of what takes place. It may be a character in the story, perhaps the central character 'speaking' in the first person. Choice of narrator is a strategy chosen by a creative writer to influence how the reader receives the story.

**official language**    a language that has a special legal status in a country, and is used in administration and education contexts.

**oral history theatre**    a general term for dramas that are created out of material spoken or written by real people. There are different kinds of oral history theatre, including verbatim theatre, which aims to edit together original words with minimum, or even no alteration.

**phonology**    the study of the sound systems of languages.

**plot**    the ordering of events in a story.

**prestige variety**    a social dialect or accent that has a high status within society.

**register**    a variety of language that is defined according to its use in particular social contexts. It is often characterised by the use of specialist vocabulary or jargon. Register can be distinguished from **dialect** in that the former is a variety defined by its uses (i.e. what one is talking about), while the latter is a variety defined by its users (i.e. who is doing the talking). For example, an academic register is the type of language use that is appropriate in academic contexts (e.g. writing essays and assignments). It will consist of the use of specialised vocabulary, a certain level of formality of expression and a particular structuring of the text (e.g. the use of an essay format, which will include an introduction, a main body built around a central argument, a conclusion, and a list of references).

**script**    a fabricated piece of spoken language (i.e. one composed by a writer) which is designed to be performed by actors.

**show**   showing and telling are two different methods of developing a story. 'Showing' allows the reader to infer what is happening; 'telling' explains to the reader what is happening.

**simile**   a figure of speech in which two different things are explicitly compared, using the words 'like', 'as', or other direct connectives (e.g. 'the colour of'); see also **metaphor**.

**sociolinguistics**   the study of language use in society. It is contrasted with general **linguistics**, which views language as an abstract system and concentrates particularly on the structure of this system. Sociolinguistics, on the other hand, examines the relationship between language and social life.

**standard language**   the variety of language that is predominantly used in broadcasting and education. A standard language does not exhibit regional variation, and is often used as the official variety within a society. It is considered to be a **prestige variety**.

**stanza**   stanza and verse are often used to mean the same thing – a section of a poem. However, 'stanza' is more commonly used of poetry, and 'verse' of song.

**stylistics**   the study of the ways in which language use produces an aesthetic, artistic or distinctive effect.

**subtext**   what characters may be thinking, despite what they are saying.

**tell**   see **show**.

**transcript**   a written representation of a piece of spoken **discourse**.

**utterance**   a complete unit of speech used by someone when speaking, and often preceded and followed by a space of silence, or by a change of speaker.

**verbatim theatre**   see **oral history theatre**.

**vernacular**   when language is 'in the vernacular', it means that the language draws on the everyday, colloquial patterns of speech, as against a more formal style of expression.

**verse**   see **stanza**.

# References

Allen, W. and Brickman, M. (2000 [1982]) *Annie Hall*, London, Faber and Faber.

Aristotle (1996) *Poetics* (trans. M. Heath), London, Penguin.

*Asahi Shimbun* (2010) 'Whale ship collides with protest vessel' [online], *Asahi Shimbun*, 7 January, http://www.asahi.com/english/Herald-asahi/TKY201001070206.html (accessed 17 March 2010).

Attardo, S. (1994) *Linguistic Theories of Humour*, Berlin, Mouton de Gruyter.

Auster, P. (1999) *Timbuktu*, London, Faber.

Bakhtin, M. (1986) *Speech Genres and Other Late Essays* (trans. V.W. McGee), Austin, TX, University of Texas Press.

Becher, T. (1981) 'Towards a definition of disciplinary cultures', *Studies in Higher Education*, 6, pp. 11–31.

Bennett, A. (1988) *Talking Heads*, London, Forelake.

Bergson, H. (2004 [1911]) *Laughter: An Essay on the Meaning of the Comic* (trans. C. Brereton and F. Rothwell), Rockville, MD, Arc Manor.

Birkner, K. (2004) 'Hegemonic struggles or transfer of knowledge? East and West Germans in job interviews', *Journal of Language and Politics*, vol. 3, no. 2, pp. 293–322.

Blake, W. (1967 [1789/1794]) *Songs of Innocence and Experience*, Oxford, Oxford University Press.

Brontë, E. (1965 [1849]) *Wuthering Heights*, Harmondsworth, Penguin.

Calvino, I. (1988 [1979]) *If on a Winter's Night a Traveller*, London, Secker and Warburg.

Campbell, S. and Roberts, C. (2007) 'Migration, ethnicity and competing discourses in the job interview: synthesising the institutional and personal', *Discourse and Society*, vol. 18, no. 3, pp. 243–71.

Chomsky, N. (1965) *Aspects of the Theory of Syntax*, Cambridge, MA, MIT Press.

Churchill, C. (1986) *Fen*, London, Methuen Drama.

Churchill, C. (1990) *Three More Sleepless Nights in Shorts*, London, Nick Hern Books.

Collins, B. (2001) *Sailing Alone Around the Room*, New York, Random House.

Collins, B. (n.d.) Interview [online], www.critiquemagazine.com/onwriting/collins_b.html (accessed 12 November 2009).

Crystal, D. (1988) *The English Language*, Harmondsworth, Penguin.

Crystal, D. (2005) *The Stories of English*, London, Penguin.

Crystal, D. (2006) 'English worldwide', in Hogg, F. and Denison, D. (eds) *A History of the English Language*, Cambridge, Cambridge University Press.

*Daily Telegraph (Australia)* (2010) 'Japanese cut in half anti-whaling ship *Ady Gil*' [online], *Daily Telegraph (Australia)*, 6 January, http://www.dailytelegraph.com.au/news/national/japanese-sink-anti-whaling-ship-ady-gil/story-e6freuzr-1225816675305 (accessed 26 July 2010).

Davis, R. (2008) *Writing Dialogue for Scripts*, London, A & C Black.

*De-Lovely* (2004) film, directed by Irwin Winkler, written by Jay Cocks, USA, MGM.

Dharker, I. (2008) 'Honour Killing', in Astley, N. (ed.) *In Person: 30 Poets*, Tarset, Bloodaxe.

Dickens, C. (1971 [1865]) *Our Mutual Friend*, Harmondsworth, Penguin.

Dickens, C. (1995 [1854]) *Hard Times*, London, Penguin.

Dooley, B. (2004) 'Doo Di Dum Di Da', *The Smoking Room*, unpublished shooting script.

Dooley, M. (1990) *Explaining Magnetism*, Newcastle upon Tyne, Bloodaxe.

*Downton Abbey* (2010) Carnival Films.

Draycott, J. (2009) *Over*, Manchester, Carcanet.

Dylan, B. (2004) *Chronicles: Volume One*, London, Simon & Schuster.

Eagleton, T. (1983) *Literary Theory*, Oxford, Blackwell.

Eliot, G. (1960 [1860]) *The Mill on the Floss*, New York, Signet.

Esling, J.H. (1998) 'Everyone has an accent except me', in Bauer, L. and Trudgill, P. (eds) *Language Myths*, London, Penguin.

Esslin, M. (1963) 'Godot and his children', in Armstrong, W. (ed.) *Experimental Drama*, London, Bell.

Fairclough, N. (2009) 'Language, reality and power', in Culpeper, J., Katamba, F., Kerswill, P., Wodak, R. and McEnery, T. (eds) *English Language: Description, Variation and Context*, Hounslow, Palgrave Macmillan.

Faulkner, W. (2004 [1930]) *As I Lay Dying*, London, Vintage.

Fitzgerald, S. (1925) *The Great Gatsby*, New York, Scribner.

Ford, F.M. (1915) *The Good Soldier*, London, John Lane.

Fordyce, T. (2009) 'England v Australia 2nd Test, Lord's, Day Five as it happened' [online], story from BBC Sport, 20 July, http://news.bbc.co.uk/sport1/hi/cricket/england/8158326.stm (accessed 26 July 2010).

Fugard, A. (1993) *The Township Plays* (ed. D. Walder), Oxford, Oxford University Press.

Gardam, J. (1992) *The Queen of the Tambourine*, London, Sinclair-Stevenson.

Gee, J.P. (2005) *An Introduction to Discourse Analysis: Theory and Method*, Abingdon, Routledge.

Gee, J.P., Hull, G. and Lankshear, C. (1996) *The New Work Order: Behind the Language of the New Capitalism*, St Leonards, Allen & Unwin.

'Get knotted! Downton Abbey talks its way into trouble with use of modern slang' (2011) http://www.dailymail.co.uk/news/article-2051332/Downton-Abbey-writers-string-language-gaffes.html (accessed 15 February 2012).

Greenwell, B. (2006) *Impossible Objects*, Blaenau Ffestiniog, Cinnamon.

Greenwell, B. (2011) *Ringers*, Blaenau Ffestiniog, Cinnamon.

Gumperz, J. (1992) 'Interviewing in intercultural situations', in Drew, D. and Heritage, J. (eds) *Talk at Work*, Cambridge, Cambridge University Press, pp. 302–27.

Gunn, T. (2007) *Selected Poems*, London, Faber and Faber.

Hall, L. (1997) *Spoonface Steinberg and Other Plays*, London, BBC Books.

Harris, B. (2009) 'Dodgers top Cards and ace Carpenter 5–3 in NLDS [online]', story from Associated Press, 7 October, http://seattletimes.nwsource.com/html/sports/2010021246_apbbncardinalsdodgers.html?syndication=rss (accessed 26 July 2010).

Harris, J. (1993) 'The grammar of Irish English', in Milroy, J. and Milroy, L. (eds) *Real English: The Grammar of English Dialects in the British Isles*, London, Longman.

Harrison, T. (2003 [1991]) 'A Cold Coming', *The Guardian*, 14 February, p. 12; also available online at www.guardian.co.uk/theguardian/2003/feb/14/features11.g2.

Hattersley, G. (1994) *Don't Worry*, Newcastle upon Tyne, Bloodaxe.

Herrington, A. (1985) 'Writing in academic settings: a study of the context for writing in two college chemical engineering courses', *Research in the Teaching of English*, 19, pp. 331–61.

Hibbert, C. (1998) *Wellington: A Personal History*, London, HarperCollins.

Hickey, R. (2007) *Irish English: History and Present-Day Forms*, Cambridge, Cambridge University Press.

Honderich, T. (2003) *After the Terror*, Edinburgh, Edinburgh University Press.

Ishiguro, K. (1989) *The Remains of the Day*, London, Faber and Faber.

James, H. (1898) *The Turn of the Screw*, London, Heinemann.

Jensen, L. (2002) *War Crimes for the Home*, London, Bloomsbury.

Jonson, B. (1947 [1641]) 'Timber: or, Discoveries', in Herford, C.H. and Simpson, P. (eds) *The Works of Ben Jonson*, Vol. 8, Oxford, Clarendon Press.

Kafka, F. (1979 [1931]) *Investigations of a Dog in Shorter Works Vol. 1*, London, Martin, Secker and Warburg.

Kane, L. (ed.) (2001) *David Mamet in Conversation*, Ann Arbor, MI, University of Michigan Press.

Komter, M. (1991) *Conflict and Co-operation in Job Interviews*, Amsterdam, John Benjamins.

Kynaston, D. (2009) *Family Britain 1951–1957*, London, Bloomsbury.

*Land and Freedom* (1995) film, directed by Ken Loach, screenplay by Jim Allen, British Screen Productions.

Laskey, M. (2008) *The Man Alone*, Sheffield, Smith/Doorstop.

Lavery, B. (2007) *Plays 1*, London, Faber and Faber.

Lippi-Green, R. (1997) *English with an Accent*, London, Routledge.

London, J. (1986 [1903]) *White Fang*, Harmondsworth, Penguin.

MacShane, F. (1986 [1976]) *The Life of Raymond Chandler*, London, Cape.

Mamet, D. (1993) *Oleanna*, London, Methuen Drama.

Mansfield, K. (1920) *Bliss, and Other Stories*, New York, Alfred A. Knopf.

McDermid, V. (1999) *A Place of Execution*, London, HarperCollins.

Mitchell, J. (1997) *The Complete Poems and Lyrics*, London, Chatto & Windus.

Murray, L. (1993) *Translations from the Natural World*, Manchester, Carcanet.

Nimmo, D. (2000) *The Wigbox*, Huddersfield, Smith/Doorstop.

Nixon, R.M. and Haldeman, H.R. (1999–2002 [1972]) 'Transcript of a recording of a meeting between the President and H.R. Haldeman in the Oval Office on June 23, 1972 from 10:04 to 11:39 am' [online] in Goldman, J. (ed.) *History and Politics Out Loud*, Evanston, IL, Northwestern University; an audio file of this transcript is also available online, http://www.hpol.org/transcript.php?id=92 (accessed 20 July 2010).

Nown, G. (ed.) (1985) *Coronation Street 1960–1985*, London, Ward Lock.

*Pierrepoint* (2005) film, directed by Adrian Shergold, written by Bob Mills and Jeff Pope, UK, Granada Television.

Pinter, H. (1991) *Plays: One*, London, Faber.

Pinter, H. (2006 [1960]) *The Caretaker*, London, Faber.

Plain English Campaign (2010) Plain English Campaign [online], http://www.plainenglish.co.uk/ (accessed 26 July 2010).

Pope, Rob (2010) 'English and creativity', in Maybin, J. and Swann, J. (eds) *The Routledge Companion to English Language Studies*, Abingdon, Routledge, pp. 122–33.

Ralph, P. (2008) *Deep Cut*, London, Oberon Books.

Roberts, C. (2010) 'Institutional discourse', in Maybin, J. and Swann, J. (eds) *The Routledge Companion to English Language Studies*, Abingdon, Routledge.

Roberts, C. and Campbell, S. (2005) 'Fitting stories into boxes: rhetorical and textual constraints on candidates' performances in British job interviews', *Journal of Applied Linguistics*, vol. 2, no. 1, pp. 45–73.

Robison, M. (1992 [1977]) 'Pretty Ice' in Ford, R. (ed.) *The Granta Book of the American Short Story*, vol. 1, London, Granta Books, pp. 434–9.

Russell, W. (2009 [1985]) *Blood Brothers*, London, Methuen Drama.

Sacks, H., Schegloff, E.A., and Jefferson, G. (1974) 'A simplest systematics for the organization of turn-taking for conversation', *Language*, 50, pp. 696–735.

Scott, W. (1862 [1817]) *Rob Roy*, Edinburgh, Adam and Charles Black.

Seger, L. (1990) *Creating Unforgettable Characters*, New York, Holt Paperbacks.

Shaw, G.B. (1960 [1907]) *Major Barbara*, Harmondsworth, Penguin.

Shaw, G.B. (1986 [1913]) *The Portable Bernard Shaw* (ed. S. Weintraub), London, Penguin.

Simpson, P. (1997) *Language through Literature*, London, Routledge.

Smith, J.J. (1996) 'Ear-rhyme, eye-rhyme and traditional rhyme: English and Scots in Robert Burns's "Brigs of Ayr"', *The Glasgow Review*, vol. 4, pp. 74–85.

Stein, S. (2003 [1995]) *Solutions for Writers: Practical Craft Techniques for Fiction and Non-fiction*, London, Souvenir Press.

Stockwell, P. (2002) *Sociolinguistics: A Resource Book for Students*, Abingdon, Routledge.

Swales, J.M. (1990) *Genre Analysis*, Cambridge, Cambridge University Press.

Swift, G. (1996) *Last Orders* London, Picador.

Swift, Jonathan (2003 [1726]) *Gulliver's Travels*, London, Penguin.

Synge, J.M. (1981 [1905]) *J.M. Synge: The Complete Plays*, London, Methuen.

Tan, A. (1990) 'Mother tongue', *The Threepenny Review*, vol. 43, pp. 7–8.

Tennyson, A. (1963 [1852]) *Selected Poems*, Oxford, Oxford University Press.

Trudgill, P. (1990) *The Dialects of England*, Oxford, Blackwell

Twain, M. (1989 [1897]) *Following the Equator: A Journey Around the World*, vol. 1, New York, Dover.

Twain, M. (1999 [1884]) *Huckleberry Finn*, Oxford, Oxford University Press.

Van Doren, C. (1919) 'Some play-party songs from Eastern Illinois', *Journal of American Folklore*, vol. 32, no. 126, pp. 486–96.

Vladimov, G. (1975) *Faithful Ruslan*, London, Simon & Schuster.

Watson, K. (2009) 'Regional variation in English accents and dialects', in Culpeper, J., Katamba, F., Kerswill, P., Wodak, R. and McEnery, T. (eds) *English Language: Description, Variation and Context*, Hounslow, Palgrave Macmillan.

Wells, H.G. (2005 [1909]) *Tono-Bungay*, London, Penguin.

Wertenbaker, T. (1988) *Our Country's Good*, London, Methuen Drama.

Whitworth, J. (2006 [2001]) *Writing Poetry*, London, A & C Black.

Whitworth, J. (2007) 'The Examiners', *The Times Literary Supplement*, 13 July, issue 5441, p. 21.

Wittgenstein, L. (1953) *Philosophical Investigations* (trans. G.E.M. Anscombe), Oxford, Blackwell.

Wodehouse, P.G. (1966) *Stiff Upper Lip, Jeeves*, London, Penguin.

Wood, V. (2007) *Housewife, 49*, Granada Television.

Woolf, V. (1998 [1933]) *Flush, a Biography*, Oxford, Oxford University Press.

# Index